JOHNNY CASH
Fighting for the Underdog

JOHNNY CASH

Fighting for the Underdog

Enslow Publishing
101 W. 23rd Street
Suite 240
New York, NY 10011
USA

enslow.com

Edward Willett

Published in 2018 by Enslow Publishing, LLC.
101 W. 23rd Street, Suite 240, New York, NY 10011

Library of Congress Cataloging-in-Publication Data

Names: Willett, Edward, 1959- author.
Title: Johnny Cash : fighting for the underdog / by Edward Willett.
Description: New York : Enslow Publishing, 2018. | Series: Rebels with a
 cause | Includes bibliographical references and index. | Audience: Grades 7-12.
Identifiers: LCCN 2017029954 | ISBN 9780766092570 (library bound)
 | ISBN 9780766095656 (paperback)
Subjects: LCSH: Cash, Johnny—Juvenile literature. | Country
 musicians—United States—Biography—Juvenile literature.
Classification: LCC ML3930.C27 W54 2018 | DDC 782.421642092 [B] —dc23
LC record available at https://lccn.loc.gov/2017029954

Printed in China

To Our Readers: We have done our best to make sure all website addresses in this
book were active and appropriate when we went to press. However, the author
and the publisher have no control over and assume no liability for the material
available on those websites or on any websites they may link to. Any comments or
suggestions can be sent by email to customerservice@enslow.com.

Portions of this book originally appeared in *Johnny Cash: "The Man in Black"* by
Edward Willett.

Photo Credits: Cover, p. 3 ABC Television/Hulton Archive/Getty Images; pp. 7,
10, 19, 68, 99 © AP Images; p. 13 Smith Collection/Gado/Archive Photos/Getty
Images; pp. 21, 24–25, 31, 38–39, 45, 55, 62 Michael Ochs Archives/Getty Images;
p. 34 Colin Escott/Michael Ochs Archives/Getty Images; p. 48 Courtesy of: The
Bill Miller Collection © Topham/The Image Works; p. 59 Pictorial Parade/Archive
Photos/Getty Images; pp. 70–71 Robert Alexander/Archive Photos/Getty Images;
pp. 76–77 Maria Bastone/AFP/Getty Images; pp. 83, 86–87 Jim Steinfeldt/Michael
Ochs Archives/Getty Images; p. 91 New York Daily News Archive/Getty Images; p.
95 KMazur/WireImage/Getty Images; p. 103 Entertainment Pictures/Alamy Stock
Photo; p. 104 Bruce Yuanyue Bi/Lonely Planet Images/Getty Images; interior pages
graphic element Eky Studio/Shutterstock.com.

CONTENTS

INTRODUCTION

Johnny Cash went to prison on January 13, 1968, not because he'd been arrested (although it wouldn't have been the first time), but to do something unique— record a live album in front of a crowd of prisoners.

Folsom Prison housed some two thousand men, including some of California's worst offenders. As they assembled in the dining hall beneath bright neon lights for the first of two shows, armed guards kept watch from overhead walkways.

Cash's new producer, Bob Johnson, suggested they forego the usual dramatic introduction. Instead, he told Cash, "All you gotta do is walk out there and jerk your head around and say 'Hello. I'm Johnny Cash.'"

It worked. The audience roared, applauding whenever they heard something they liked—such as Cash's songs about prison and crime, loneliness and separation. Five tape machines captured their noisy appreciation, and from those tapes came one of the best live albums ever made.[1] It sold six million copies and reached number

Johnny Cash plays live at California's Folsom Prison in January 1968. The performace was recorded for a special live album, which went on to sell more than three million copies during Cash's lifetime.

thirteen on the pop charts. The equally popular *Johnny Cash at San Quentin* followed. In 1969, Johnny Cash sold more records in the United States than the Beatles.

Johnny Cash already had a reputation as a rebel. *Johnny Cash at Folsom Prison* solidified it. But he was a rebel with a cause: ordinary people.

1

Born into Hard Times

Johnny Cash experienced the struggles of everyday people firsthand: he was born in Kingsland, Arkansas, during the depths of the Great Depression.

His father, Ray Cash, from nearby Rison, met Carrie Cloverlee Rivers in 1919, when he was twenty-two and she was fifteen, while boarding with her family while he was cutting lumber. They married on August 18, 1920. Their first son, Roy, was born in 1921, and was followed by Margaret Louise in 1924 and Jack in 1929.

When their third son came along on February 26, 1932, Carrie wanted to name him John, after her father. Ray wanted to name him Ray. Unable to agree, they compromised on J.R.

Ray was a sharecropper, renting his land by sharing his crop with the landowner. On October 29, 1929, the stock market crashed, triggering an economic collapse. Banks failed, businesses closed, and more than 15 million Americans, one quarter of the workforce, lost their jobs.[1]

Between 1928 and 1932, the price of a 500-pound bale of cotton dropped from $125 to $25,[2] and as a result, Ray Cash could no longer make a living as a sharecropper. He took whatever work he could find: cutting wood at a sawmill, clearing land, laying railroad track, painting, shoveling, herding cattle.[3] When he couldn't find work, he

Photos of Johnny Cash as a child are displayed in the old Dyess Colony in Dyess, Arkansas, Cash's childhood home. The property was turned into a museum in 2014.

hunted small game like rabbits, squirrels, and opossum to feed his family.

Sometimes he rode the rails, traveling in boxcars, picking fruits and vegetables all over the country. "Our house was right on the railroad tracks. . .and one of my earliest memories is of seeing him jump out of a moving boxcar and roll down the ditch in front of our door," Cash wrote in his second autobiography in 1997.[4]

After President Franklin D. Roosevelt announced his New Deal, Ray Cash applied, answering questions covering everything from the family's debts to their church preference, farming experience, and club affiliations. The initial decision to reject his application was reversed, and on March 23, 1935, the family climbed aboard a truck that would take them and their belongings to Dyess, 250 miles away over narrow, muddy roads. Ray and the three boys rode in the back under a tarpaulin, Carrie and the two girls (J.R.'s second sister, Reba, was born in 1934), in the cab. Johnny Cash said the first song he remembered singing was "I Am Bound for the Promised Land," bouncing in the back of the truck.[6]

On March 24, the family arrived at House 266: five rooms, no plumbing or electricity, with a barn, a mule, a chicken coop, a smokehouse, and an outdoor privy.[7] For the Cashes it really did look like the Promised Land.

THE NEW DEAL

Elected in 1932, President Franklin D. Roosevelt promised a "New Deal" to help Americans. He established the Federal Emergency Relief Administration, which created a program to relocate needy families to brand-new, model communities.

Colonization Project Number One would later be called Dyess, after an Arkansas government administrator. Built on 16,000 acres of reclaimed swampland, it boasted a town hall, a movie theater, a cotton mill, a cannery, churches, a cotton mill, shops, a school, and a hospital. Each relocated family would receive a brand-new house, twenty acres of land to clear and farm, a barn, a mule, a milk cow, and a hencoop.[5]

Early Days in Dyess

The Dyess families grew their own food, along with cotton, which they sold collectively, sharing in any profits. While Ray and Roy cleared the land, the three younger children played and Carrie gardened, canning her fruits and vegetables at the community cannery for the coming winter. Government home economists taught canning, cooking, dressmaking, and other skills. Children received regular medical check-ups.[8]

Ray made his annual payment of $111.41 promptly every year. He also paid off the annual advance payment he received on his crops. By 1940, he was able to purchase the farm next door, giving him forty-five acres. By 1945, he owned both house and land.[9]

He almost lost everything in January 1937, when the nearby Tyronza River flooded. Carrie and the younger children were evacuated to Kingsland. Ray and Roy had to flee after a week. When the Cashes returned on February 16, silt covered their house, snakes infested the barn, hens had laid eggs on the sofa, and driftwood littered the land. But they cleaned up and carried on, and the silt improved the soil: Ray's crop yields increased.

The First Notes

In 1938, J.R. got a new sister, Joanne, and started school. He also began helping in the cotton field, first just carrying water, but later picking cotton alongside his father and brothers, stuffing it into a six-foot-long canvas sack.

In Dyess, people sang—as they worked, and in church. In Road Fifteen Church of God, which J.R. attended with his mother, guitars, mandolins and banjoes sometimes accompanied the gospel songs.

A battery-operated radio in the house played church music on Sundays and country music the rest of the week, and J.R. liked to listen to it. Ray thought he was wasting his time, but Carrie loved music, playing piano in church and singing to the children. Her father had taught singing, and she wanted her family (now including another son, Tommy, born in 1940) to have music in their lives.[12]

A home in the Dyess Colony in 1935. Johnny Cash and his family lived in a similar house in the Dyess community for impoverished farmers during Cash's childhood.

FATHER KNOWS BEST

Ray Cash was a harsh taskmaster. Cash biographer Michael Streissguth writes that when Roy, J.R.'s oldest brother, made a mistake or was impertinent, his father would whip him with the leather reins from the mule.[10]

Johnny Cash said his father never laid a hand on *him*, but admitted to verbal and emotional abuse: when J.R. was five years old, Ray shot the stray dog that had become his pet, and didn't tell the boys until they found the body. He claimed the dog had been eating scraps intended for the hogs.

"I thought my world had ended that morning, that nothing was safe, that life wasn't safe," Johnny Cash wrote in his second autobiography. "It was a frightening thing, and it took a long time for me to get over it."[11]

"We sang in the house, on the porch, everywhere," Johnny Cash remembered. "We sang in the fields. . .I'd start it off with pop songs I'd heard on the radio, and my sister Louise and I would challenge each other: 'Bet you don't know this one!' Usually I knew them and I'd join in well before she'd finished."[13]

J.R.'s big brother Roy even played in a band with four schoolmates, the Delta Rhythm Ramblers. The band won a local talent contest in 1939, but just two years later the Second World War began, and all the members were drafted.

Roy joined the Navy, and with him gone, J.R.'s next-oldest brother, Jack, became his mentor.

Tragedy

J.R. idolized Jack: he seemed tougher and smarter and more Christian than everyone else, already talking about becoming a Baptist minister. "There was nobody in the world as good and as wise and as strong as my big brother Jack," Johnny Cash wrote.[14]

J.R. went to church twice on Sundays and attended Bible study every Wednesday night. On February 26, 1944, just after J.R. turned twelve, the "age of accountability," with the congregation of First Baptist Church singing "Just As I Am," he walked down the aisle to the front of the church to give his life to Christ. Jack, sitting in the front row, watched as his little brother took the preacher's hand, then knelt at the altar. "It was like a birthday rolling around," Cash wrote in his first autobiography. "I felt brand-new, born again."[15] He also felt closer to Jack than ever before.

But then came Saturday, May 12, 1944.

J.R. decided to go fishing. He asked Jack, but Jack was heading to the school workshop to earn some money cutting fence posts. They walked together for a little bit, then separated.

Around noon, J.R. headed for home. A Model A Ford met him, with the preacher driving and Ray with him. Ray told J.R. to throw away his fishing pole and get in, then told him Jack had been pulled onto the circular saw in the workshop. The blade had ripped into his stomach.

Jack lingered a few days. On May 20, he asked his mother whether she could hear the angels singing. Then he told her he could hear them, and that was where he was going. And then he died.

"I felt like I'd died, too," Cash wrote later. "I was terribly lonely without him. I had no other friend."[16] Worse, his father blamed *him*, telling him he should have died rather than Jack, that he had no business fishing while Jack was earning money to help the family.[17]

And yet, the tragedy, guilt, and unfair accusations had one positive outcome: they kick-started J.R.'s creativity. "It's when I started writing," he wrote. "I was trying to put down what I was feeling."[18]

Birth of the Music

C arrie Cash had bought a guitar from Sears & Roebuck before Jack died, but it was sold to pay the doctor's bills and offset the loss of income from Jack's work. But J.R. still wanted to learn to play, so he turned to a classmate, Jesse "Pete" Barnhill. Because his right hand had been withered by polio, Pete played his Gibson flattop guitar by chording with his left hand and just beating the rhythm with the other.[1]

"Pete was crazy for music the way I was," Cash wrote, "and we were both crazy for the radio."[2] Together, they'd sing songs by country artists like Hank Snow, Ernest Tubb, and Jimmie Rodgers.

J.R.'s mother thought his voice was a gift from God. "She was determined that I was going to leave the farm and do well in life," Cash wrote.[3] She signed him up for music lessons, working a full day doing laundry to earn the $3 each lesson cost.

J.R. decided music lessons were all right when he discovered his teacher, LaVanda Mae Fielder, of nearby Lepanto, Arkansas, was young and pretty. But halfway through the third lesson, after listening to J.R. sing popular ballads like "I'll Take You Home Again, Kathleen," Fielder closed the piano and asked him to sing a song *he* wanted to sing, without accompaniment.

J.R. sang Hank Williams's "Long Gone Lonesome Blues." When he finished, Fielder told him to never take voice lessons again. "Don't let me or anyone else change the way you sing."[4]

"I was pretty happy about that," Cash said. "I didn't really want to change. I felt good about my voice."[5]

He quit lessons, but kept singing during long evening walks back to the house. "It was pitch black on the gravel road, or if the moon was shining, the shadows were even scarier," he wrote. "But I sang all the way home. . .I sang through the dark, and I decided that that kind of music was going to be my magic to take me through all the dark places."[6]

Teenage Years

J.R. was popular in high school. According to Louise Nichols, his first girlfriend, "Everybody loved him. Everybody!"[7]

Sue Moore, who dated J.R. when he was a senior and she was fifteen, said, "I thought he was a hunk."[8]

Nadine Johnson, whom he *also* dated that year, said, "I think what attracted me to him was that he was so well-liked."[9]

But sometimes, his friends noted, J.R. was "kind of off on another planet."[10]

"It seemed like he was going somewhere," remembered his friend A.J. Henson. "He was on a journey."[11]

Most of the kids in Dyess wanted to go somewhere else. The post-war economic boom was creating manufacturing jobs in the big cities, and returning World War II veterans told tales of the wider world. "It was second nature that we

Johnny Cash, then going by J.R. Cash, in his high-school yearbook photo. Cash was the vice president of the class of 1950 at Dyess High School.

wouldn't live in Dyess when we were grown," Cash wrote. "It was the aim of every person to get a better job."[12]

In his senior year, J.R. was elected class vice-president and an officer in the school's chapter of the Future Farmers of America, not that he intended to be one. At his graduation on May 19, 1950, he performed "Drink to Me Only with Thine Eyes."

At that point, he could only play a couple of chords on the guitar, and had only seen two live concerts: the Louvin Brothers, who'd performed in the high-school auditorium, and the Grand Ole Opry in Nashville, which he'd attended on a school trip.

In Nashville, he saw the Carter family perform, and was particularly taken with the youngest Carter daughter, a girl named June.[13]

A Working Man

Done with school, Cash hitchhiked to Bald Knob, Arkansas, and picked strawberries for three days. Then, like thousands of other Southerners, he boarded a bus and headed north to the automobile factories of Michigan. With him were a barber from Dyess, Frank Kinney, and a school friend, Milton Stansbury. They arrived in Pontiac, Michigan, about midnight, went down to the Fisher Body plant at 8 a.m. to apply for jobs, and at 4 p.m. went to work.

Cash earned a $1.50 an hour stamping metal into car hoods, but hated the work. Three weeks into the job, he cut his right forearm, quit, and returned to Dyess. For two weeks he worked with his father at the Proctor and Gamble margarine factory in nearby Evadale.

Then, on June 25, 1950, North Korea invaded South Korea. Within a few days, American troops were involved in combat.

Enlistment. . .and Vivian

Every boy had to register for the draft at the age of eighteen. Being drafted meant you had no choice as to which branch of the service you served in. If you volunteered, you could choose.

Johnny Cash poses for a portrait in 1955 in Memphis, Tennessee.
Later that year, Cash would release his first songs with Sun Records,
"Hey Porter" and "Cry! Cry! Cry!"

To avoid being drafted into the infantry, Cash travelled to Blythesville, Arkansas, on July 5, and enlisted in the Air Force for a four-year stint. When asked for his first and last name, he wrote in John Ray Cash, and he soon ceased to be J.R. and became John, or Johnny.

Cash was formally inducted into the Air Force on July 7, 1950, in Little Rock, Arkansas. Later that summer he took a train from Memphis, Tennessee, to San Antonio, Texas, to begin his training at Lackland Air Base.

Cash had an aptitude for listening to and transcribing radio transmissions, so after two months of basic training, he was sent to Keesler Air Force Base in Biloxi, Mississippi, to study Morse code, typing, and electronics. From there, he was recruited by the newly formed Twelfth Radio Squadron Mobile (RSM).

After graduating from Keesler on April 27, 1951, Cash took eight weeks of advanced training at Brooks Air Force Base in Texas. One day at the roller-skating rink, he met a pretty seventeen-year-old Italian girl, Vivian Liberto. For the rest of his stay, they dated.

After a month's leave in Dyess, Cash headed north to meet up with the rest of the Twelfth RSM before boarding a ship for West Germany.

Listening to the Soviet Union

After landing in Bremerhaven, in northern Germany, the Twelfth RSM travelled by train to Landsberg, a town of about 10,000 people near Munich, in the southern part of the country.

Cash and his colleagues in the Twelfth RSM worked eight-hour shifts in a windowless room on the top floor of a three-story building, earphones clamped to their

POST-WAR GERMANY

The Second World War had only been over for six years, and as they travelled, the Americans saw collapsed bridges, the blackened ruins of factories and houses, and bombed-out churches. Their destination, Landsberg, had never been bombed, but there were eleven concentration camps in the area, and Adolf Hitler had written *Mein Kampf*, the book that gave rise to the Nazi party, while imprisoned in Landsberg in the 1920s. War criminals were still being held and executed in that same prison. Cash's air base was a former Luftwaffe (German Air Force) base. Travelling through post-war Germany must have been an eye-opening experience for the young man from rural Arkansas.

heads, straining to hear, above the static, the encrypted messages in Morse code coming from the Soviet Union and its satellite nations, including Soviet-occupied East Germany. They passed the results to analysts to decipher. Cash, as one of the unit's most capable operators, was soon promoted to staff sergeant.

True to his strict upbringing, at first Cash neither drank nor socialized with those who did. Instead, he

Johnny Cash plays the guitar while his first wife, Vivian Liberto, looks on in 1957. Later that year, Cash would become the first Sun Records artist to release a long-playing album.

spent a lot of time playing and singing old songs with other homesick soldiers. Many were accomplished musicians. Playing with them, Cash improved his own guitar playing.

He also started writing his own songs, including his first gospel song, "Belshazzar," and "Hey! Porter," which was published in the military newspaper *Stars and Stripes*.

"Sometimes I am two people. Johnny is the nice one. Cash causes all the trouble. They fight."– Johnny Cash

Practically everybody in Germany drank beer. Before long, so did Cash. "I took a part in most everything else that goes along with drunkenness that last year in Germany," he would later write.[15] Nevertheless, he continued regularly attending chapel, praying each day, and reading the Bible.[16] He kept writing songs, and played with a group called the Landsberg Barbarians.

On leave, Cash visited Paris, Venice, Zurich, London, Salzburg, Amsterdam, and Berlin. And all the time he was writing letters to Vivian Liberto, the girl from the roller-skating rink, sometimes two or three a day.

Back to the States

Cash returned to the US early in the summer of 1954. He was honorably discharged on July 3, and married Vivian on August 7, in San Antonio.

Cash had found a job and an apartment in Memphis, where his brother Roy, sister Reba, and others from Dyess had moved. He sold appliances door-to-door for the Home Equipment Company, but he'd made up his mind in Germany that he was going to be a musician.

One way to break in was through radio, so Cash applied for an announcer's job in Corinth, Tennessee, eighty miles east of Memphis. Station director John Bell told him that with his twangy Arkansas accent he'd never make it without more training, and suggested Keegan's School of Broadcasting in Memphis. For ten months, Cash took lessons two mornings a week.[17]

In September 1954, Cash and Vivian moved into a two-bedroom, second-floor apartment with a private bathroom but a shared kitchen. Within a few months, Cash had made enough money as a salesman that he and his then-pregnant wife moved to a larger apartment.

Music in Memphis

Despite his sales success, Cash wrote later, "I spent more time in my car listening to the radio than I did knocking on doors."[18] And he wasn't just listening. Roy had introduced him to two automobile mechanics, Marshall Grant and Luther Perkins, who also played guitar and sang. "We'd sing and play until the early hours of the morning, night after night," Cash said.[19]

The trio began to think about making a record. To improve their sound, Perkins switched to lead electric guitar and Grant to bass. Cash, who did most of the singing, stuck to rhythm guitar. After four months of rehearsing, they gave their first public performance in a Memphis church, then played a fundraiser for Ralph Johnson, a powerboat racer and friend of Grant's who'd been injured in a collision.

They made their first money, $50, playing on the back of a flatbed truck cruising Union Avenue, advertising the

A HIT IS BORN

Cash's iconic hit "I Walk the Line" was born in West Germany one day when Cash discovered someone had been playing with his tape recorder. On the tape he heard strange sounds, including a voice that seemed to say, "Father."

It turned out someone had put a tape on the recorder upside down and backwards while recording guitar chords. What Cash heard as "Father" was "turn it off," backward.

That upside-down and backward chord progression on the tape "broke all the musical laws in history," Cash said—but it eventually became "I Walk the Line."[14]

Hurst Motor Company. For three months they played (for free) every Saturday on KWEM Radio, sponsored by Cash's employer, Home Equipment.

Their number of live engagements grew, but what they really needed was a record.

Sun Records Rises

Sam Phillips had launched Sun Records in 1952, renting a small space at 706 Union Avenue in Memphis. The city swarmed with musicians, and they played everything from boogie-woogie and western swing to gospel, blues, and hillbilly. Phillips would record anyone he thought was good.

In 1954, Phillips discovered Elvis Presley, whose success attracted many other artists—not just Johnny Cash, but also Carl Perkins, Jerry Lee Lewis, and, later, Roy Orbison, Bill Justis, and Harold Jenkins (better known as Conway Twitty).[20] Phillips liked drums, almost unheard of in country music at the time, and his preferred style of sparse instrumentation with a strong, drum-driven rhythm became the hallmark of "rockabilly," a forerunner of rock.

"I was fully confident that I was going to see Sam Phillips and to record for him," Cash recalled. "When I called him, I thought, 'I'm going to get on Sun Records.' So, I called him. . .and he turned me down flat."

Two weeks later, Phillips turned him down again. Cash wanted to record gospel songs and Phillips didn't think they would sell. Finally, Cash took his guitar to the studio, sat on the front step, and waited. When Phillips arrived, Cash said, "I'm John Cash. I'm the one that's been calling. And if you'd listen to me, I believe you'll be glad you did."[21]

Phillips did listen, and on a Thursday afternoon in May 1955, the same month Cash's daughter Rosanne was born, Cash, Perkins, and Grant recorded "Hey! Porter!"

For the flip side, Phillips had asked for "a love song, or maybe a bitter weeper."[22] Cash wrote "Cry, Cry, Cry." Phillips liked it so much he released it first. He suggested Cash call himself "Johnny" instead of "John," so the trio dubbed itself "Johnny Cash and the Tennessee Two."

Grant wrote that when he heard their record played on the radio one morning while driving to work, "I thought that was *it*."[23] But the next day, five Memphis stations were playing their song. The day after that, all of them were. By the end of the week, they were playing both sides. After a month, stations across the South were playing Cash's song, and the record climbed to number fourteen on the country music charts.

Offers for live gigs started rolling in. Cash wrote to his friend Ted Freeman in late July that a potential manager, Bob Neal, thought they could play five or six nights a week right through the winter, making at least $20 a night—$30 or more in larger towns. "I believe I can make a pretty good living at it," he wrote, and signed himself "Johnny Cash—the most promising young artist Memphis, Tennessee, has ever produced."[24]

3

Here Come the Hits

Bob Neal, a disc jockey for the WMPS radio station in Memphis, who also owned a record shop, had been promoting and emceeing country music shows since the beginning of the decade. In December 1954, he took over management of Elvis Presley. (Not for long: By the next summer, Colonel Tom Parker had mostly taken over, and went on to make Elvis a superstar.)

Neal created a booking agency, Stars Incorporated, to book Sun Records artists. Among the first to sign were Johnny Cash and the Tennessee Two. By June 1956, Neal had become Cash's personal manager.

Cash vs. Elvis

Cash and Elvis Presley had a friendly rivalry, keeping tabs on each other's record sales and concert successes, and even mimicking each other in their performances.

A turning point in both their careers came at Overton Park Shell in Memphis on August 5, 1955, a concert that featured twenty-two acts and drew more than 4,000 fans. The last time Elvis had played there he'd been billed under Slim Whitman. In their debut, Johnny Cash and the Tennessee Two were billed far below Elvis.

They performed "Cry, Cry, Cry" and "Hey! Porter!" and encored "Folsom Prison Blues," which they'd recorded but not yet released. . .then watched Elvis perform while "the girls and women screamed, cried, and fainted."

"He had. . .a personal magnetism on and offstage—but especially onstage—that is unique," Cash remembered.

The only newspaper photos of the show were of Elvis Presley. . .and Johnny Cash.

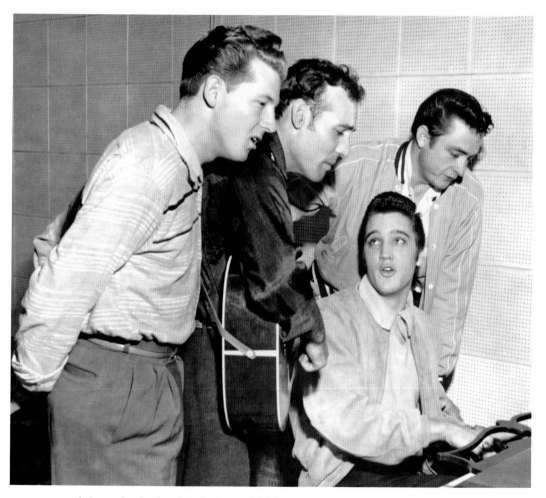

Johnny Cash (far right) plays with The Million Dollar Quartet, featuring (from right) Jerry Lee Lewis, Carl Perkins, and Elvis Presley for one night only in 1956.

Through Sun Records, Cash met Carl Perkins, famous for "Blue Suede Shoes," who became one of his "longest, truest" friends. One night backstage at a show in Gladewater, Texas, which Elvis was headlining, Cash was playing with the peculiar riff he'd heard on the twisted tape in Germany. He told Perkins he was writing a song called "Because Your Mine" about being true to himself, his wife, and God. He sang the first verse.

"'I Walk the Line' would be a better title," Perkins said.

"The lyrics came as fast as I could write, and in twenty minutes I had it finished," Cash remembered.

At that show and others, audiences loved Elvis, but didn't know what to make of Cash and the Tennessee Two. "People would stand there and look at you with the mouth open because they hadn't never heard anything like us, because there hadn't been anything like us," Marshall Grant said.

Rockin' on the Radio

Louisiana Hayride, broadcast weekly on KWKH radio out of Shreveport, Louisiana's Municipal Auditorium, could be picked up as far west as California and was sometimes carried by CBS and Armed Forces Radio. It had helped launch Elvis Presley's career, and it helped launch Cash's. His two performances on December 3 drew standing ovations. Cash called the reaction "intoxicating," and signed to appear every Saturday night for a year.

On December 15, 1955, Sun Records released "Folsom Prison Blues."

"There was nothing like it in popular music," Cash biographer Michael Streissguth wrote. "Compared to Presley's exuberance, Perry Como's urbane whispers, and

A FATEFUL DECISION?

The day after his debut on *Louisiana* Hayride, a Sunday, while riding in the car with Grant and Perkins, Cash felt a pang when he realized he should be in church. Grant offered to stop at one, but Cash decided they should keep driving because they had to get to a show. He later said his decision left him "vulnerable and easy prey for all the temptations and destructive vices that the backstage of the entertainment world has to offer." Though it is unlikely that missing church that morning caused all his problems, Cash would later go on to abuse alcohol and drugs, and would suffer the unhappy end of his first marriage.

the Drifters crooning harmonies, Cash and the Tennessee Two's 'Folsom Prison Blues' was rope burn. . .jagged and raw. . .an unflinching look at an ugly place."[1]

In January 1956, just a few weeks before turning twenty-four, Cash received a royalty check from Sun for $6,000, more than his father had ever earned in a year.

He quit his day job.

The Memphis music scene shot to national prominence that year. Elvis Presley's contract had been purchased by RCA late in 1955, and his first RCA single, "Heartbreak Hotel," was number one on the charts by April. Carl

Sam Phillips, the founder of Sun Records, presents Johnny Cash with a framed "I Walk the Line" record to commemorate a sales milestone in May 1956.

Perkins's "Blue Suede Shoes" was number four in March, the first song in history to simultaneously hit the pop, country, and R&B charts.

For Cash, "Folsom Prison Blues" was a top-ten country hit. On April 2, 1956, Cash and the Tennessee Two recorded four more tracks, including "I Walk the Line." Cash recorded it as a slow ballad, but Sam Phillips convinced him to pick up the tempo on a late take—and then sent that version to radio stations.

"When I heard it, I called Sam and asked him not to send out any more because it sounded so awful," Cash said. "But that's the one everybody liked, so all of a sudden I started liking it, too."[4]

"I Walk the Line" reached number one on Billboard's country music charts and eventually sold more than two million copies.

Cash bought a bigger house and a better car. His little brother Tommy, still in high school in Dyess, remembered that suddenly they had become "Johnny Cash's family." Instead of people asking him about his basketball, or his dad about the cotton harvest, they'd want to know how Johnny was, and when his new record would be out.[5]

A 'Grand' Debut

On July 7, 1956, with "I Walk the Line" climbing the charts, Cash achieved another long-held ambition, appearing for the first time on the Grand Ole Opry, country's most prestigious showcase.

In the *Nashville Banner*, Ben A. Green wrote that "I Walk the Line" unleashed a "veritable tornado" of applause. "The boy had struck home, where the heart is," and the country audience "had taken a new member into

FOLSOM PRISON PLAGIARISM?

Johnny Cash wrote "Folsom Prison Blues" in Germany, lifting the melody, and a lot of the words, from Gordon Jenkins's song "Crescent City Blues." [2]

When the *Johnny Cash at Folsom Prison* album came out, Jenkins filed a lawsuit, eventually settling out of court for almost $100,000. Cash readily admitted that he'd borrowed heavily from the other songwriter's work—but he claimed his intent was not to harm Jenkins. He never even imagined anyone would hear his version of the song when he first wrote it.

"I really had no idea I would be a professional recording artist," Cash said in 1996. "I wasn't trying to rip anybody off." [3]

the family." An unnamed "veteran Opry Official" said, "He's one of us." [6]

But Cash didn't like the way the Opry tried to tie him down to pure country, or the way some of the old-timers thought he was too "rock and roll"—and that rock and roll was for black people. Cash told *Rolling Stone* in 1992 that when he left that night, he told himself, "I don't wanna go back. . .I don't have to put up with this crap." [7]

Still, the Opry had introduced him to June Carter, during that high-school field trip, and on the night of his debut, June, her mother, and her two daughters were performing as the Carter Family. Backstage, Cash joked to June that one day he'd marry her. She replied, "Good. I can't wait."[8]

"I can't remember anything else we talked about, except his eyes," she wrote decades later, "those black eyes that shone like agates."[9]

Meanwhile, Cash's wife, Vivian, had just given birth to their second daughter, Kathy.

On the Road

That year, Cash and the Tennessee Two traveled to Colorado, Arizona, Pennsylvania, Ohio, and Minnesota. In December, in California, Ralph J. Gleason wrote in the *San Francisco Chronicle* that "if the reaction of the crowd at the performances is any indication, Presley has a rival."[10]

The California tour had been booked by Stew Carnall, who figured so many Midwesterners had moved to California during the Depression and war years that there had to be a market for country music. When Cash proved him right, he bought half of Cash's management contract for $5,000, plus seven percent of Cash's next annual gross, becoming Cash's tour manager. In April 1957, thanks to Carnall's management, Cash and his band left the US for the first time, touring Canada for twenty-four days.

Cash began to appear on TV shows, including a ten-show commitment to the popular *Jackie Gleason Show*. Journalist Robert Johnson said that was the "magic door" that swung open to give Cash "a chance at the

Cash — with a personalized acoustic guitar — performs onstage in 1957. That year, Cash and his band, The Tennessee Two, toured the United States and Canada to promote his new album.

glory road": Gleason Enterprises had helped Elvis reach national prominence.[11]

Cash and the Tennessee Two had to drive themselves to shows, and get back to Shreveport almost every Saturday night for *Louisiana Hayride*. Cash wrote to his friend Ted Freeman in May 1957, after the tour of Canada, that they had averaged 420 miles per day, that he was twenty-six pounds lighter and ten years older, and that "I AM TIRED and sick."[12]

Two months later, during a tour with Patsy Cline, Ray Price, Ferlin Husky, Faron Young, and Hank Thompson, Young's fiddle player, Gordon Terry, gave Cash a small white tablet.[13]

The pill was a "Benny": Benzedrine, an amphetamine, prescribed for everything from fatigue to obesity. It provided a burst of energy and euphoria and confidence, but restlessness and fatigue followed. You slept away most of the next day—or took another pill to keep going.

That first pill woke Cash up so well that at show time in Jacksonville, Florida, he took another one. "They left me exhausted, but I had discovered something I sincerely thought would be a good thing for me," Cash later wrote.[14]

Late in 1957, Cash, Vivian, and their daughters, Rosanne and Kathy, moved into a new house on Walnut Grove Place in Memphis. But Cash wasn't there much: he was spending more and more time in California, appearing regularly on the Saturday-night Los Angeles TV program *Town Hall Party*, where he met Tex Ritter, Merle Travis, and Johnny Western. Ritter recorded traditional cowboy music, while Travis was best known for a recently re-released album of folk songs (two of which, "Dark as a Dungeon" and "John Henry," Cash would make a standard part of his repertoire in the 1960s). Johnny Western, who would later join Cash's road show, specialized in Western ballads. Together, they reawakened Cash's interest in the songs of the Old West.

Meanwhile, Cash and the Tennessee Two were increasingly unhappy with Sam Phillips. He'd featured Cash on the first Sun Records album, *Johnny Cash with His Hot and Blue Guitar*, but they thought he was focused too much on his "next big thing," Jerry Lee Lewis.[15] They even suspected Phillips was holding back some royalty money, though that was never proven.[16]

Cash later said that what really made him unhappy was Phillips's refusal to let him record more gospel music: "That didn't sit well with me, and when I started thinking in terms of other hard-sell music, I got more restless still."[17]

Farewell to Phillips

On August 13, 1957, Columbia Records producer Don Law met Cash backstage at *Town Hall Party* and asked if he'd consider signing with Columbia when his Sun Records contract expired in July 1958. Law told Cash he'd let him record a gospel album, and would be willing to discuss other hard-to-sell ideas. After further negotiations, Cash signed.

Phillips heard about it and asked if it were true. Cash said no. Phillips said later, "I knew when he opened his mouth he was lying. The only damn lie that Johnny Cash ever told me that I was aware of. That hurt. That hurt!"[18]

"I don't know why I found it easy to lie to Sam about it," Cash wrote, "but that's how it was."[19]

Phillips threatened to sue Columbia for contractual interference, and to sue Cash if he didn't record the rest of the songs his Sun contract required. Cash returned to Sun in May 1958, but rather than record his own material, he sang some Hank Williams songs and some written by the engineer, Jack Clement.

With his Memphis ties severed, Cash moved to California. Perkins and Grant didn't like it and soon moved back to Tennessee, reuniting with Cash only for concerts or recordings.

Up the Ladder of Success

After a short time in a Hollywood apartment, the Cash family, now including Cynthia (Cindy), moved to a new house in Encino. As *Time Magazine* noted in 1959, in just four years, Cash had sold more than six million records, and noted that his latest, "Don't Take Your Guns to Town," was well on its way to repeating the million-plus sales of "I Walk the Line."[20]

"Don't Take Your Guns to Town," the story of a young cowboy killed in a shootout after he ignores his mother's pleas to leave his guns at home, hit just as Westerns were taking off in movies and on TV. It reached number one on the country charts and stayed there for six weeks. It also climbed the pop charts. Eight more Cash songs came out in 1958, four from Columbia and four from Sun, which still had plenty of Cash recordings tucked away.

"Don't Take Your Guns to Town" was also featured on Cash's first Columbia album, *The Fabulous Johnny Cash*, one of three albums released in 1959; the others were *Hymns by Johnny Cash*, his gospel album, at last, and *Songs of Our Soil*, a collection of folk songs.

Among the songs on the non-gospel albums were two biographer Michael Streissguth calls the "finest nuggets" Cash mined from his past: "Pickin' Time," about a poor farmer hoping for better times when the harvest is done, and "Five Feet High and Rising," inspired by the flood when Cash was five years old

"The choice to transform Depression stories into mass entertainment made Cash unique," wrote Streissguth. In contrast to the lightweight, feel-good pop of the era, Cash was "digging up the country's thick and tangled roots."[21]

Bob Dylan, who would soon make his name as a folk singer, heard Cash on the radio when he was a high-school student in Hibbing, Minnesota. "It was different from anything else you had ever heard," he wrote after Cash's death. "The record sounded like a voice from the middle of the earth. It was so powerful and moving. It was profound."[22]

Cash continued to tour, assembling *The Johnny Cash Show*. Johnny Western and various female vocalists joined him, including Rose Maddox, Patsy Cline, and, in 1962, thirteen-year-old Barbara Mandrell. Cash liked to drive, to the alarm of cast members. "He was the world's worst driver," Johnny Western remembered. "Patsy Cline wouldn't ride if he was driving."[23]

Cash needed superhuman energy to get everything done. Increasingly, he got that energy from amphetamines.

4

Sliding Downhill

"My friends made a joke out of my 'nervousness,'" Cash wrote in his 1975 autobiography. "I had a twitch in the neck, the back, the face. My eyes dilated. I couldn't stand still. I twisted, turned, contorted, and popped my neck bones."[1]

Some of his friends knew the truth: Marshall Grant saw Cash taking pills backstage late in 1957. But even those who didn't couldn't ignore Cash's increasingly erratic behavior or weight loss—or the concerts cancelled because of laryngitis, a side effect of amphetamines.

Vivian Cash knew. "She saw them as deadly right from the start," Cash wrote, "when she'd get up in the morning. . .and there I'd be, wide-awake and red-eyed after staying up all night in the den, writing and singing and putting things down on tape."[2]

By the time Cash, Vivian, and their three daughters moved to California, his marriage was in trouble. "My kids suffered—Daddy wasn't there for school plays, Fourth of July picnics. . .my absence was a loss that can never be made up."[3]

Eventually, everyone around Cash knew he was on drugs. Yet he kept the shows coming. Grant recalled

Singer Johnny Horton (left) and Cash pose for a photo in Kingsland, Arkansas, in 1959. Horton, one of Cash's closest friends, passed away just a year later after a fatal car accident.

JOHNNY HORTON

By 1960, Cash sometimes didn't go home between tours, instead travelling to Shreveport, Louisiana, to spend time with his close friend Johnny Horton and his wife, Billie Jean. When Horton died in a car accident in 1960, Cash flew to Shreveport to console Billie Jean. Not long after the funeral, he flew her to New York for a three-week shopping spree, canceling concerts to do so. He arranged her finances for her, and even gave her funds to tide her over until she got money from Horton's final hit recording, "North to Alaska."

"We were close," Billie Jean said years later, "but the only thing that put the kibosh on it was the drugs. Had he not been on the pills, trust me, I would have married him."[5]

leading Cash out on stage when the singer didn't even know where he was, but "the crowd would stand up screaming and hollering for five minutes, (and) by the time that was over with, the guy could do a show. And do a good show."[4]

In November 1961, Cash and another man were arrested at 3:30 a.m. in Nashville after Cash attempted to kick down the door of a club. It was closed, but he thought it was just refusing to let him in.

Stew Carnall became Cash's sole manager in 1961, buying out Bob Neal. But in May, Cash also hired a promoter from London, Ontario, Saul Holiff. Previously an unofficial advisor on Cash's frequent Canadian tours, Holiff impressed Cash by getting an improved contract out of Columbia.

Holiff coined the phrase "America's foremost singing storyteller." He booked concerts at the Hollywood Bowl and Carnegie Hall. (The latter was a disaster: amphetamines had dried out Cash's voice so much he could barely sing). But what turned out to be Holiff's most important contribution was hiring June Carter to join *The Johnny Cash Show*, beginning with a performance that December in Dallas.

The Johnny Cash Show

In the fall of 1961, Cash moved his family (now with a fourth daughter, Tara) to a new, isolated home on fifteen hillside aces north of Ventura, California. Rosanne Cash remembers it as "horrible."[6]

By that point, no one knew why Cash did anything. Strung out on drugs, he was both "one of the greatest human beings who ever walked on the face of this earth"

Johnny Cash with June Carter in 1964. Cash first met June backstage at the Grand Ole Opry in 1955, and she was a close companion throughout the 1960s, until they wed in 1968.

and "the greatest jerk that ever lived," in the words of Marshall Grant.[7]

Everyone knew Cash had to get off drugs, but only June Carter did anything about it. She'd seen some of the same behavior from the late Hank Williams when the Carter Family had toured with him, and she didn't want to relive the experience.

June had already been married twice, from 1952 to 1955 to country star Carl Smith, with whom she had one daughter, and then in 1957 to Nashville police officer Rip Nix, with whom she had another daughter. She had been limiting her touring to look after her children, but now she began spending more time on the road with *The Johnny Cash Show* to look after its star.

June would hunt for Cash's pills while he slept and flush them down the toilet. "She once told me that if she had a dollar for every pill of Johnny Cash's that she'd flushed, none of us would ever have to work again," wrote John Carter Cash, the son she'd eventually have with Cash. "She loved him, and she wanted him to succeed— and most of all, to survive."[8]

She and Marshall Grant would stay up all night with Cash "just to keep in touch with him, to keep him alive and stop him from hurting anybody." Neither could have done it alone, Grant said. "We could barely do it together."[9]

June didn't just want Johnny Cash clean of drugs, she wanted Johnny Cash, and the feeling was mutual. "Within months of meeting, the relationship between June and Cash became a full-blown affair," wrote Cash's authorized biographer, Steve Turner. They kept it discreet, though. Both were still married, and Cash's public image was a devoted family man.[10]

49

"RING OF FIRE"

When June started collaborating with Merle Kilgore, who'd written the hit "Wolverton Mountain," June told him she was "torn apart" because she was so in love with Johnny Cash, and the first song they wrote together was called "Promised to John."

Then she read Kilgore a letter from a friend who had just gotten a divorce, in which one phrase stood out: "I hate love. Love is like a burning ring of fire."

Kilgore seized on that metaphor, which also seemed to describe June's feelings about Cash. The resulting song, originally called "Love's Burning Ring of Fire," was recorded by Anita Carter and released in November of 1962. Cash told June he'd wait four months to give the original version time to succeed before he recorded it.[11]

Searching for a Hit

Cash needed a hit: he hadn't had a single on the pop charts for nearly four years. Only two of his last twelve had even reached the Top 100, and of all his albums, only *The Fabulous Johnny Cash* had made the Top 20. "His records weren't selling and he was in bad shape," is how Kilgore put it. And his Columbia Records contract was due to expire at the end of 1963.

Kilgore suggested Cash ask his old Sun Records engineer, Jack Clement, to help produce his version of "Ring of Fire." Cash told Clement he'd dreamed about the song having trumpets in it. Trumpets were unheard of in country music, but Clement went out and hired two trumpet players just the same. He played guitar himself.

"Success is having to worry about every damn thing in the world, except money."
– Johnny Cash

"Ring of Fire," released in May 1963, reached number seventeen on the singles charts, and a new "best-of" album, also called *Ring of Fire*, made it to number twenty-six on the album charts. Cash's Columbia contract was renewed.

A Marriage Crumbles

Cash and June Carter recorded "The Legend of John Henry's Hammer" together in June 1962. Later that month they recorded the first song they co-wrote, "The Matador." A few weeks after that, Cash was a special guest at a Carter Family recording session.

Vivian Cash knew something was going on. She had brought the children and Cash's parents, Ray and Carrie, to Cash's Hollywood Bowl show. Afterward, Kathy Cash remembered, "We were standing there waving good-bye to Dad, and he kissed us all, got into his car, and then June [with Luther and Marshall] jumped into the car right next to him and waved to us. Mom was furious. . .That was when she started falling apart."[12]

On the rare occasions Cash came home, Kathy lay awake listening to her parents fight. Vivian wanted a husband who was home more often, physically and mentally. For his part, Cash recorded "Understand Your Man" in November 1963, obviously directed at Vivian.

Cash thought June, who neither drank nor used drugs, both understood him and was a steadying influence.

A Folk Foray

The musical spotlight was swinging toward folk as young people sought "authenticity." In New York City, Cash met Peter La Farge, who in 1961 had recorded "The Ballad of Ira Hayes," the story of a Pima Indian, one of the six US marines photographed raising the US flag on Iwo Jima during the Second World War, who had died, a poverty-stricken alcoholic, in 1955. The song pointed out that Hayes had fought for his country, but his ancestral land did not have enough water.

Cash recorded the song in March 1964. Some country music DJs refused to play it because they considered it too controversial. Cash then built a whole concept album, *Bitter Tears*, around the plight of Native Americans. The *New York Times* praised it as "one of the best LPs to emerge from the '60s folk movement."[13]

Cash sang "The Ballad of Ira Hayes" at the Newport Folk Festival on July 25, 1964. He'd been exchanging letters with Bob Dylan, and at Newport they spent a night taping songs in a local motel with Joan Baez and her sister and brother-in-law, Mimi and Richard Farina. Two days later, Cash and his band recorded a first take of Dylan's "Mama You've Been on My Mind." Later that summer, Cash and June recorded Dylan's "It Ain't Me Babe," which made it to the top five of the country charts and crossed over to the pop charts.

Over the next year, Cash recorded other people's folk songs ("Orange Blossom Special" scaled both the country and pop charts), wrote his own protest song, "All of God's Children Ain't Free," and recorded a two-disc album, *Johnny Cash Sings Ballads of the True West*. It was too expensive for most buyers, but a single-disc version released in 1966 reached number four on the country charts.

But all the time, the drugs were eating away at Cash. At the Grand Ole Opry in 1965, unable to free a microphone, Cash lost his temper and dragged the stand across the footlights, sending glass flying into the audience. The Opry banned him.[14]

It was just one sign that Johnny Cash was about to hit rock bottom.

5
Down and Out and Up Again

Late in September 1965, Cash and the Tennessee Three (drummer W.S. "Fluke" Holland had joined in 1960) were supposed to play "I Walk the Line" to open the finale of a "Nashville in New York" edition of CBS-TV's *Steve Lawrence Show*—but Cash was so strung out, he couldn't perform.

Then, after the last show of a Texas tour, Cash missed his flight from Dallas to Los Angeles. Instead he went to El Paso, took a cab to Juarez, Mexico, and bought socks stuffed with amphetamines.

On October 4, two narcotics agents arrested him at El Paso International Airport. Cash was thrown in jail. At his bond hearing, which Cash later called the "public documentation of the low point of my entire career," the singer snarled at reporters and threatened to kick one photographer's camera out of his hands.

Two months later, Cash returned to El Paso for his arraignment. He pled guilty to possession of illegal drugs, and was given a thirty-day suspended sentence and fined $1,000. He'd stayed clean for six weeks after being released from jail, but by the arraignment he had returned to what he called "my shadows of death—the pills."[1]

In March 1966, in front of 3,000 people, he wandered barefoot onstage at Toronto's O'Keefe Centre, in Holiff's words, "very, very, very strung out." Holiff cancelled the show.[2]

In May, Cash flew to London for a tour of the British Isles. He met up again with Bob Dylan, also on tour, and attended one of his shows. Holiff, with a great deal of difficulty, had lined up a prestigious show for Cash at the Olympia Theatre in Paris to immediately follow the British tour—but Cash, partying with Dylan, failed to show up at the airport. Furious, Holiff flew back to the States.

Cash went home briefly, then headed off on yet another tour. When it ended, he didn't go home at all, instead

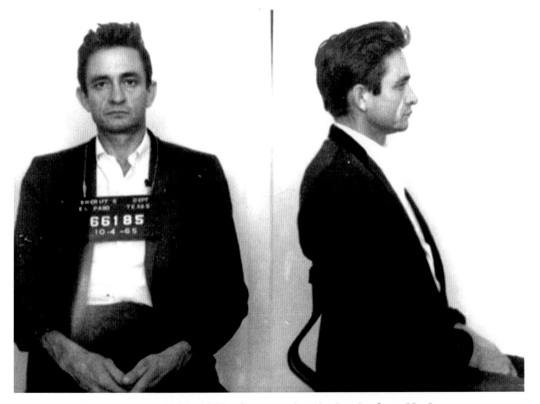

Cash was arrested in 1965 after crossing the border from Mexico into the United States while in possession of hundreds of pills and tranquilizers. Cash called the embarrassing incident the lowest point in his entire career.

staying with his friend Gene Ferguson in Brentwood, California. Vivian and June Carter kept calling Ferguson to see if Cash was there. At Cash's request, Ferguson lied and said he wasn't.[3]

An End—And a Beginning

On June 30, 1966, Vivian filed for divorce, citing "extreme cruelty" and "grievous mental suffering and anguish." Worried Cash would sell their communal property or conceal some of his earnings, she got a court order to prevent him and, not knowing where he was, had it published four times in the *Nashville Banner* in August 1966. Cash was ordered to appear in court on August 22 in Ventura, California, but didn't show. On August 29, his attorney denied that Cash had shown extreme cruelty, inflicted grievous mental suffering, or had any intention of concealing his wealth or disposing of any property.

As negotiations continued, Kathy Cash asked her mother what a divorce would mean. Vivian said the only difference would be that "Daddy's clothes would no longer be hanging in the closet."[4]

Cash quit contesting the divorce on August 30, 1967. Vivian received custody of the children, $400 a month (plus medical care and insurance) per child, $6,500 to pay her attorney's fee, and a substantial financial settlement.[5]

As the proceedings wound down, Cash bought a new house overlooking Old Hickory Lake in Hendersonville, Tennessee, north of Nashville—his home for the rest of his life.

Struggling to Stay Clean

Cash just couldn't seem to kick his drug habit. Marshall Grant estimates that by 1967, fully half of Cash's shows were being cancelled, which meant promoters didn't want to book him. In a telegram, Holiff warned Cash, "Your professional behavior is totally reprehensible, showing a complete disregard for the rights and feelings of everyone around you."[6]

What saved Cash wasn't concern for his career, but love. Divorced, he could finally marry June Carter. . .but she said she'd only marry him if he got off drugs.

Cash told different stories about how he turned his life around. In his 1997 autobiography, and other interviews in the nineties, he said he entered Nickajack Cave near Chattanooga, intending to get lost in it and starve. Instead, he said, he felt a "great comfortin' presence" telling him that he wasn't going to die, that "I got things for you to do." He said June and his mother were waiting for him when he emerged, and as they drove him back to Nashville he told them he was ready to recommit his life to God and kick his drug habit.[7]

But in his first autobiography in 1975, Cash puts the turning point on the night he spent in jail in Lafayette, Georgia, in October 1967.

Sheriff Ralph Jones had arrested Cash after he knocked on the wrong door in the middle of the night, frightening a woman. Rather than charge Cash with disorderly conduct, he asked Cash why he would throw away his career and his family for the sake of getting stoned. "I just felt led to say that to him," he said later.[8]

In that account, Cash wrote that he got in a car with a friend, Richard McGibony, and said, "You'll never see me high on dope any more."[9]

Whatever the truth, he agreed, at June's urging, to meet with psychiatrist Nat Winston. He told Winston he'd been taking twenty or thirty amphetamine capsules at a time, three or four times a day, followed by twenty or so tranquilizers a night to try to get some rest. One-on-one counseling and a concerted effort to keep the pills away from Cash followed, but as Cash himself wrote in 1997, his "liberation from drug addiction" wasn't permanent. "Though I've never regressed to spending years at a time on amphetamines, I've used mood-altering drugs for periods of varying lengths of times since 1967: amphetamines, sleeping pills, and prescription painkillers."[10]

Still, he'd turned a corner. On November 11, 1967, Cash performed a benefit concert for Hendersonville High School to raise money for new band uniforms. It was the first time he had performed drug-free in more than a decade, and he discovered it wasn't as frightening as he'd thought. Relaxed, joking with the audience, he amazed himself.[11]

And then, in January of 1968, came *Johnny Cash at Folsom Prison*.

A One-of-a-Kind Recording

In the tumultuous 1960s, anything "anti-establishment" was cool, and what could be more anti-establishment than an album recorded in a prison? So Cash took his "Folsom Prison Blues" to the song's namesake prison and recorded an album live, with an audience of inmates looking on.

Critic Greg Kot called it "one of the best live albums ever made and a country music landmark."[12]

Cash's good luck continued through the year. On February 22, 1968, Cash proposed to June Carter, live on stage in London, Ontario. They were married a little over a week later at the Methodist Church in Franklin, Kentucky. In between, they flew to Hollywood to collect a Grammy Award for best country-and-western performance by a duo for "Jackson."

Cash also found a religious reawakening. "God had done more than speak to me," he wrote in his 1997

Johnny Cash and June Carter Cash perform together in 1979. The pair toured together many times over the years, starting with the Carter Family band in the 1960s.

59

autobiography. "He had revealed His will to me through other people, family and friends. The greatest joy of my life was that I no longer felt separated from Him."[13] His next album, *The Holy Land*, combined new gospel songs with comments and thoughts Cash and June recorded as they toured Israel shortly after their marriage.

But 1968 had its bad side, too. In early August, Luther Perkins fell asleep on his sofa while smoking. The sofa ignited. Perkins died of burns two days later.

Perkins had asked Cash to come over and Cash had refused. Perkins had been drunk, and Cash also felt responsible for contributing to his chemical abuse. "A part of me died with Luther," Cash told an interviewer ten years later.[14]

Carl Perkins filled in for Luther for a few shows, but when a flight delay kept him from a show in Fayetteville, Arkansas, Cash called up a guitarist from the audience, Bob Wootton from Tulsa, Oklahoma, who said he had memorized the guitar part on every Johnny Cash recording. A local bass player filled in on bass. Bob Wootton would go on to play with Cash for most of the next thirty years.[15]

Back to Prison

In early 1969, Cash recorded *Johnny Cash at San Quentin*. The concert was filmed by the UK's Granada Television for a documentary. "A Boy Named Sue," written by Shel Silverstein (author and illustrator of *Where the Sidewalk Ends*, and other children's poetry books), the first song released, reached number two on singles chart, Cash's best showing ever, but he was a little annoyed it was for a song someone else wrote.[16]

At the concert, after Cash encored with "San Quentin," the prisoners were standing on tables, screaming. Ralph Gleason, a concert reviewer for *Rolling Stone*, said, "If he had screwed up one notch higher the joint would have exploded."[17] But instead Cash calmed things down, then played a less aggressive version of the song. (He later claimed that he was tempted to say, "Let's do it," and unleash a riot.[18])

Johnny Cash at San Quentin was even more popular than the Folsom Prison recording, because Cash now had his own television show.

Johnny on TV

The Granada Television documentary aired in Britain in April 1969, before the album released, and proved to ABC television executives just how charismatic Cash could be. They offered him his own show as a summer replacement for *Hollywood Palace*. Holiff agreed, provided Cash could film in Nashville's Ryman Auditorium (home of the Grand Ole Opry), and the producer was Stan Jacobson, who had made a 1967 TV special for CBC TV in Canada.

For the moment, Cash's addiction was under control. "Any time he wanted to come back down he could do it," Marshall Grant wrote. He put on weight, and by the time the show started filming, he "looked excellent."[19]

The show rehearsed Mondays, Tuesdays, and Wednesdays. Tapings (usually two shows a week) were on Thursdays. Cash performed concerts on the weekends. Though Cash claimed he'd never liked television, now he said, "if I'm going to have to do it every day, I might as well enjoy it."

Folk singer Bob Dylan plays along with Cash during an appearance on the popular *The Johnny Cash Show*, filmed in Nashville, Tennessee, in 1969.

He added, "I like my guests,"[20] and it was those guests who made *The Johnny Cash Show* unique. Cash showcased performers rarely seen on TV. His opening show featured Bob Dylan and Joni Mitchell. Merle Haggard, Buffy St. Marie, Mama Cass, Gordon Lightfoot, and Linda Ronstadt followed. None were as famous then as they would become. All were from the folk, blues or country worlds, rather than pop.

Cash soon ran afoul of the network brass. He wanted Pete Seeger as a guest, but Seeger was a former Communist and anti-war activist. "Pete Seeger is a great American," he complained to the director, Bill Carruthers. "Why can't I have my friends on?"[22] The network relented, but in exchange, Cash had to mix in guests like Bob Hope and Phil Harris, whose style of entertainment had little

AN IRISH LAD DISCOVERS CASH

Among the many viewers Cash impressed was Paul David Hewson, a nine-year-old boy in Ireland—better known today as Bono, lead singer for the band U2.

Bono has called *The Johnny Cash Show* "an amazingly generous act, a great gift to the world," that moved people like Dylan from the fringe to the center of the entertainment world.[21]

Twenty-five years later, Bono would help move Cash back "from the fringe to the center of the entertainment world."

to do with his own. Still, viewers liked what they saw, and ABC picked up the show for seventeen more episodes, beginning in January 1970.

In each show, Cash sang some well-known songs and duets with guests and with June, then finished with a gospel song with the Carter Family and the Statler Brothers. Second-season guests included Ray Charles, Judy Collins, Roy Orbison, Roger Miller, and Waylon Jennings.

A filmed segment, "Ride This Train," focused on American life or history: religion, prisons, hobos, cotton picking, trains, the Wild West. Cash, often in period costume, would talk directly to the camera. It became his favorite part of the show.

Success on network TV helped rehabilitate Cash's image with viewers, who forgave the stories from just a couple of years before of missed shows, broken footlights, and illegal drugs. As Kris Kristofferson, a guest in 1970, said, "By the time he did his TV show he was such a figure of stability. It was like he was the father of our country."[23]

In real life, Cash was the father of a new son, John Carter, born in March 1970. Having a son helped Cash battle his addiction and renewed his focus on spirituality. He befriended evangelist Billy Graham, appearing with the Carter Family and the Statler Brothers at a Graham youth revival in Knoxville, Tennessee, on May 24, 1970, where he talked about his drug abuse. "It ain't worth it," he said. He later called the appearance "the pinnacle of my career."[24]

"You Can't Say That on Television"

The Johnny Cash Show was renewed for a full twenty-six-episode third season, starting in September 1970. But on

November 18, 1970, Cash, against the advice of producer Stan Jacobson, made an explicit statement about his Christian beliefs. Jacobson warned he risked alienating part of his audience. Cash wrote later that he knew Jacobson was right, but he felt he had to "let the chips fall where they may," because he'd been getting thousands of letters from people asking him if he was a Christian, and he felt he had to take a stand.[25]

"After that statement, the show took a nose dive," Jacobson said. The network began trying stunts, even making Cash do a mini-special at a circus, but nothing worked. The program ended for good in March 1971. Cash heard the news while touring in Australia. NBC invited him to move to their network, but Cash refused. He seemed more relieved than anything else. [26] "Television steals your soul," he told one reporter.[27]

THE MAN IN BLACK

One song written for *The Johnny Cash Show* was "Man in Black." Cash, who had been wearing mostly black outfits for years, had previously given three reasons: it stayed clean longest, it was good for wearing in church, and it was easy to coordinate.

But in "Man in Black," he claimed he wore black in remembrance of sorrow and injustice. The song's title became one of Cash's best-known nicknames.

However, Cash didn't only wear black. As he once explained, "I wear black because I'm comfortable in it. But then in the summertime when it's hot I'm comfortable in light blue."

Cash never regretted speaking up. "If you were in my shoes and believed what I believe, you'd have been a fool to choose a decade or two's worth of record sales over eternal salvation."[28]

Cash was an international celebrity now. He'd appeared in a western with Kirk Douglas, *A Gunfight*. He had a new son. He made an estimated $3 million a year. He had a beautiful home surrounded by 146 acres of land. He had a newfound commitment to his faith. He was clean of drugs. He was at a career high point.

Which meant, as always with Cash, there was only one way to go: down.

6

Rock Bottom

The decline in Cash's career this time was gradual, as he simply carried on as he had been—including focusing even more strongly on religion.

On May 9, 1971, Cash answered the altar call at Evangel Temple, an Assembly of God church in Madison, Tennessee. The preacher, Jimmy Snow, son of country music legend Hank Snow, had made it his mission to have a Christian impact on country music. He later said, "It is one thing for a public figure to join a church. It is another thing for him to humble himself to get down on his knees and crawl and cry in front of a congregation."[1]

"I don't have a career anymore," Cash said afterward. "What I have now is a ministry."[2]

A spate of religion-themed projects followed. *Gospel Road*, a ninety-minute movie about Jesus's life, was filmed in Israel through November 1971, directed by Robert Elfstrom, who also portrayed Jesus. June played Mary Magdalene. Reba Hancock, Cash's sister, played the Virgin Mary. Jimmy Snow played Pontius Pilate, and Saul Holiff played the high priest Caiphas. A group of European backpackers played the twelve apostles. Cash sang his own songs and songs by Larry Gatlin, Kris Kristofferson, John Denver, and others.

In 1971, Cash produced a film on the life of Jesus Christ, filmed at the Sea of Galilee, in Israel. Although Cash did not appear in the film, he narrated the feature and recorded the soundtrack.

Despite a lot of media attention and a very positive review in *Newsweek*, *Gospel Road* made little splash at the box office, and the associated album only reached number twelve on the country charts. "Children," the sole single, only made number thirty.

Still, biographer Michael Streissguth praises the effort. "Few, if any of his peers had stepped from their regular recording careers to pursue a new genre, and the fact that Cash did so is a tribute to his continued desire to challenge himself by reaching for new spheres."[3]

Unfortunately, Streissguth notes, "America's arbiters of chic rejected it."[4] *Rolling Stone* ran an extensive profile of Cash after the movie came out, but made no mention of the film or the album.[5]

Singing the Gospel

Cash did more and more religious concerts, notably at Explo '72, sponsored by Campus Crusade for Christ. More than 150,000 people attended the closing concert at an abandoned racetrack. Billy Graham called it a "religious Woodstock."[6]

Cash played a similar event in 1973 at London's Wembley Stadium. He performed on Jimmy Snow's *Grand Ole Gospel Hour*, broadcast from Nashville's Ryman Auditorium after the Grand Ole Opry show, and performed for other evangelists, including Oral Roberts.

He continued to make frequent television appearances, not just as a singer, but as an actor; for instance, he played a dishonest evangelist on NBC's detective show, *Columbo*. He was so well known that President Richard Nixon invited him to the White House.

But *The Gospel Road* didn't sell. *The Junkie and the Juicehead Minus Me*, featuring singers from his family (including June's daughters Carlene Smith and Rosey Nix, and Cash's daughter Rosanne) did even worse; in 1974, neither of its two singles made it onto the charts.

For 1975, trying to boost sales, Columbia asked Cash to record an album of new songs by young songwriters, but it, too, was a failure. Only "The Lady Came from Baltimore," written by Tim Hardin, made it onto the country charts, topping out at number fourteen. Cash's most powerful numbers had always

been the ones he wrote himself, but he wasn't writing anymore.

Johnny and June Carter perform at a memorial concert in honor of
A.P. Carter, June's cousin and the founder of the Carter Family band,
in August 1977.

Nor was he seen as "counter-cultural" any longer. "He used to write a lot of good songs before he started hanging out with the wrong company there at the White House," was how folk singer Phil Ochs put it. Waylon Jennings said Cash had "sold out to religion."[7]

In 1972, Cash had released a concept album entitled *America: A 200-Year Salute in Story and Song*, and in 1974 he'd hosted a TV special, *Ridin' the Rails*, the story of America's railroads. That made him a natural fit for many of the celebrations surrounding the United States' Bicentennial in 1976, so his profile remained high.

But Saul Holiff thought he saw the writing on the wall. He retired as Cash's manager. Lou Robin took over. Holiff said, "I truly believed that it was going to be anticlimactic from then onward, and it was. For the next ten or twelve years he went into a tailspin."[8]

Not that the tailspin was obvious. Cash hosted a TV special and a four-episode run of *The New Johnny Cash Show*. He received a star on Hollywood boulevard. On July 4, the 200th anniversary of the signing of the Declaration of Independence, he was Grand Marshall for the Bicentennial Parade in Washington, D.C., which included a concert in front of the Washington Monument.

Although the title track of his 1976 album *One Piece at a Time* was his biggest hit in years, topping the country charts and reaching number twenty-nine on the Top 40 pop chart, flagging album sales continued to worry Cash. He talked about doing an album based on his Sun Records days, with songs by Elvis Presley, Carl Perkins, and Roy Orbison, but instead he recorded *The Rambler*. Based on old-time radio shows, it told the story of a man wandering the highways. It flopped.

Down and Out

Not only that, but according to Marshall Grant, by 1976, Cash was back on drugs, and his habit was worse than ever.[9] By 1977, he'd switched from attending Evangel Temple to the Hendersonville Church of God. Soon he stopped going to church there, too. (Still, in May 1977, he received an associate of theology degree after completing—with straight A's—an intensive Bible-study correspondence course with the Christian International School of Theology, and he continued performing at Billy Graham rallies.)

On August 16, 1977, his old rival Elvis Presley died. An autopsy revealed eleven different drugs in his bloodstream. It might have served as a wake-up call to Cash—but it didn't.

June Carter's mother, Mother Maybelle Carter, died October 22, 1978. Sara Carter, the last survivor of the original Carter Family, died three months later.

Cash's recording career seemed to be dying, too: his 1978 album *Golden Girl* didn't even make the country charts. The following year, Columbia released *Silver*, celebrating Cash's twenty-fifth anniversary (a year early). In 1980, his *real* twenty-fifth anniversary year, Cash brought out *Rockabilly Blues*. Both albums contained excellent work. Neither made much impact.

Silver was the last album featuring Marshall Grant. He called the last few years with Cash, after he was back on drugs, "a living hell."[10]

"There was no excuse for it," he wrote. "I'm seventy-five years old and I've never tasted a drop of alcohol." After he left the show, Cash got even wilder. "June couldn't do anything with him and no one else cared."[11]

In June 1981, Grant filed a $2.6 million lawsuit, charging Cash with breach of contract and slander. Relatives of Luther Perkins also claimed his estate was owed money. Both cases were settled out of court.

Despite their conflict, Grant would later say that, near the end of Cash's life, the two men reconciled.[12]

To rejuvenate his career, Cash surrounded himself with younger producers and musicians, including his daughter Rosanne, whose own album, *Seven Year Ache,* had gone gold, and June's daughter Carlene, wife of British musician Nick Lowe, a central figure in New Wave pop music.

But, Cash noted in his second autobiography, "Sometimes in the early '80s I really cared about recording, but sometimes I didn't. . .Periodically, someone took the initiative and suggested something new or different to turn the situation around, but nothing ever worked."[13]

He kept touring, and in 1981 appeared in the critically acclaimed CBS movie *The Pride of Jessi Hallam,* about adult illiteracy. But he was simply riding on the coattails of his own previous success.

A Bizarre Attack

After eye surgery in 1981, Cash became addicted to prescription painkillers, an addiction worsened after a bizarre incident that September, when he was attacked by an ostrich in his personal animal park in Hendersonville

"Waldo," possibly upset by the death of his mate, kicked Cash, breaking two of his lower ribs and ripping open his abdomen. "If the belt hadn't been good and strong, with a solid buckle, he'd have spilled my guts," Cash later wrote. Cash broke three more ribs when he fell on a rock.

He kept taking his painkillers when he no longer needed them for pain, seeking out multiple doctors to prescribe them. The painkillers upset his digestive system, so he started drinking wine, which also took the edge off the amphetamines he'd resumed taking. As he later put it, he was "up and running, strung out, slowed down, sped up, turned around, hung on the hook, having a ball, living in hell."[14]

As if that weren't enough, during the Christmas season in 1981, while he, June, their eleven-year-old son John Carter, and other guests were at Cinnamon Hill, the

RAY CASH

Cash's father, Ray, died on December 23, 1985.

Cash had moved his parents into a house near his own near Hendersonville, and often praised them in concerts for working so hard to put him through school and encouraging him to go out and sing. He always dedicated the song "These Hands" to Ray.

But in his 1997 autobiography, Cash wrote that whenever he made that dedication he could hear his father's presence protesting, "I didn't encourage you."

"He was right, of course," Cash wrote. "His attitude had always been, 'You won't amount to a hill of beans.'"[18]

"He never once told me he loved me. . .It would have meant an awful lot for me to have heard it, just once, before he died."[19]

Cash receives the Grammy Legend Award in 1990, surrounded by his family, (from left) son Johnny Carter Cash, wife June, daughter Roseanne, and son-in-law Rodney Crowell.

Cashes' vacation house in Jamaica, three masked and armed men broke in, held everyone hostage for four hours, and fled in June's Land Rover with $50,000 worth of stolen goods.

The thieves were soon caught. Two were jailed and later died trying to escape. The third was killed resisting arrest. Jamaican Prime Minister Edward Seaga personally apologized to the Cashes.

On November 10, 1983, Cash's cocktail of painkillers, amphetamines, tranquilizers, and liquor caught up with him. In Nottingham, England, near the end of a European tour, he tried to pull a fold-up bed from his hotel room's wall—but the room didn't have a fold-up bed. He tore up the wall and tore up his hands, too, driving splinters into his right hand, which became so badly infected it had to be operated on in Nashville. The doctors also discovered internal bleeding, and operated to remove his

"THE CHICKEN IN BLACK"

One of the last singles Cash recorded for Columbia was "The Chicken in Black," a song about a bank-robbing Johnny Cash that clearly parodied his hit "The Man in Black." In the video, Cash wore a superhero's blue cape, yellow jersey, and tights.

"It was intentionally atrocious," Cash claimed in his second autobiography. "I was burlesquing myself and forcing CBS to go along with it."[22]

But in 1988 he told *Musician* magazine he'd hated the song from the first day: "It was an embarrassment."[23]

damaged duodenum and parts of his spleen, stomach, and intestines. Cash had taken his own stock of drugs into the hospital with him, and post-surgery they also put him on morphine, which gave him intense hallucinations.[15]

Cash's family arranged for him to be admitted to the Betty Ford Center, a drug addiction treatment center in Rancho Mirage, California. When he emerged forty-three days later, his friends saw an enormous change. He was "so sober and lucid all the time," said Karen Robin, the wife of Cash's manager Lou Robin.[16]

It didn't last. "Now I know where to go to get help," Cash wrote in 1997, but "I've gone and got it several times since that first awakening. . .because my problem persists."[17]

The Hits Keep on Comin'

Cash wrapped up a 1984 European tour with a Christmas special in Montreaux, Switzerland, with special guests Waylon Jennings, Willie Nelson, Kris Kristofferson, Toni Wine, Connie Nelson, and Jessi Colter. That led to Cash, Jennings, Nelson, and Kristofferson forming The Highwaymen. The name came from a 1977 song by Jimmy Webb, which they recorded, along with others, at impromptu recording sessions back in the States, producing a ten-song album, which made it number one, as did the title song.

The Highwaymen toured several times and made two more recordings, but never recaptured that initial success.

Cash's solo efforts continued to go nowhere. Work on his own album, *Rainbow*, was held up for *The Highwaymen*, and then for an album of duets with Waylon Jennings, and then for a return to Sun Records for *The Class of '55*, released by Polygram, which also featured Carl Perkins, Roy Orbison, and Jerry Lee Lewis. When *Rainbow* finally did come out, neither it nor any of its tracks made it onto the charts.

Lou Robin blamed Columbia for giving it no promotion[20]; it seemed the record company no longer believed Cash was worth much, and sure enough, when his contract expired in the spring of 1986, it wasn't renewed.[21]

On August 21, 1986, Cash signed a new contract with Polygram to record on its Mercury label. His first album,

Johnny Cash Is Coming to Town, reunited him with his old Sun Records engineer Jack Clement. Mercury promoted *Johnny Cash Is Coming to Town* as Cash's comeback album, but neither it nor its two singles made much of an impact on the charts.

Water from the Wells of Home, an album of duets, did even worse.

And then Cash's health crashed again. In 1988 he underwent cardiac bypass surgery, and contracted pneumonia. He managed to perform again in March of 1989, but two months later he was back in a hospital in Paris, France, with chest pain. Throat problems plagued him over the next few months, and just before Thanksgiving, he checked into another drug and treatment center.

In January 1990, a dentist removed an abscessed tooth. A cyst developed that had to be scraped away. It weakened Cash's jaw, and in March, he broke it. The surgery to fix that left the bottom half of his face disfigured, damaged the nerve endings around the bone, and resulted in constant pain he compared to a blowtorch being held to his jaw.

Johnny Cash seemed to be nearing the end of his career. . .but once again, appearances were deceiving.

7

A New Audience

Cash's mother, Carrie, died on March 11, 1991, at the age of eighty-six. Cash biographer Steve Turner said Cash's mother was "the biggest single influence on his life," encouraging him in both his music and his faith. When she died, Cash cried publicly for the first time anyone could remember.[1]

Cash's US concerts no longer drew sell-out crowds (though people still flocked to see him in Europe), and his health made touring difficult. He decided to set up shop in Branson, Missouri, where other fading and/or aging country stars had taken to performing regularly for tourists. Cash agreed to lend his name to Cash Country, to be designed and built by David Green, a California property developer. Cash was to perform seventy-five nights a year in one of the $35-million, hundred-acre entertainment complex's three 2,500-seat theatres.

Cash Country, set to open May 1, 1992, was also supposed to include a horse arena, a go-kart track, an amusement park, a water park, a museum (modeled on the existing Johnny Cash Museum in Hendersonville, which had opened in 1979), a hotel, three motels, and a shopping mall. But work stopped in the spring of 1991, and by November, Green was bankrupt.

Instead, Cash signed on for fifty shows at the 3,000-seat Wayne Newton Theater. Some nights, only a few hundred people would show up. The theater manager thought Cash seemed ambivalent and disinterested.[2]

With Cash Country failed, Cash had to go back on the road. On February 8, 1993, he was in Dublin, Ireland, where Bono invited him to record lead vocals for "The Wanderer," the final track on U2's album *Zooropa*.

Zooropa topped the charts in both Britain and the US, and sold more than seven million copies worldwide. Suddenly, a whole new generation of listeners discovered Johnny Cash.

Just two weeks after his return from Dublin, after a show in Santa Ana, California, Cash met with record

CASH AND BONO

As noted earlier, Bono had been a fan of Cash since he was a little boy, but they met in person for the first time in 1988, at Cash's home in Hendersonville.

Bono recounted how Cash said "the most beautiful, poetic grace" at the dinner table, thanking God for the food. "Then, when he was done, he looked at me and Adam Clayton and said, 'Sure miss the drugs, though.'"[3]

Bono called Cash "a saint who preferred the company of sinners," a deeply religious man who nonetheless embodied all the excesses associated with superstardom.[4] That intrigued Bono, and led to the *Zooropa* invitation.

producer Rick Rubin, the thirty-year-old owner of Def American Records, who had produced such acts as LL Cool J, the Beastie Boys, Run DMC, Slayer, and the Red Hot Chili Peppers. To Cash, Rubin looked like "the ultimate hippie," with his untrimmed beard, long hair, and "clothes that would have done a wino proud," and Cash didn't take him seriously.

"I was through auditioning for producers, and I wasn't at all interested in being remodeled into some kind of rock

Johnny Cash (second from left) poses with producer Rick Rubin (third from left) and others backstage at Los Angeles's Greek Theatre in 1997.

act," he wrote, although he did tell June that he thought Rubin talked "a little like Sam Phillips."[5]

The two kept talking, though, discussing possible songs for a potential album. Occasionally they met in the informal recording studio in Rubin's Los Angeles home so Cash could play songs. The meetings went so well, and Cash was so impressed by Rubin's stated intent to let him be "totally honest," that Cash agreed to sign with American Records.[6]

"Johnny was made fun of in Nashville for working with me," Rubin said. "It seemed ridiculous to that audience. But he saw the seriousness of what we talked about and could do together—enough to go against those feelings."[7]

Back to Basics

American Recordings, released in 1994, featured just Cash and his acoustic guitar, singing more of his own compositions than he had on almost any of his albums of the previous twenty years.

The first single was an old ballad about murder called "Delia's Gone." With lyrics updated to include submachine guns, it linked American folk music with gangsta rap. In the accompanying, controversial video, Cash tied up model Kate Moss, threw her into a pit, and shoveled dirt over her face. Before the album's release, Cash appeared in fashionable nightclubs and at the ultra-hip South by Southwest music festival in Austin, Texas.

Critics raved. "I don't think I lost any of my old fans, and I might have gained a few new ones," Cash wrote.[8]

American Recordings reached number twenty-three on the country music charts—Cash's highest position in sixteen years. It won him his first Grammy Award (for Best Contemporary Folk Album) since 1969.

But in other ways, Cash's career continued to decline. The Johnny Cash Museum closed in 1995, after sixteen years. The House of Cash, the gift shop near Cash's home, had cut back to ten employees from forty. Soon, it, too, would close.

For his second album with American Records, *Unchained*, Cash and Rubin added a backing band— Tom Petty and the Heartbreakers, whom Rubin had first produced in 1994 for the album *Wildflowers*. This album included songs from many contemporary songwriters,

BACK ON THE ROAD

His road shows took on new life. Playing in "young people's places," he said, "I discovered all over again how it felt to play for a crowd of people with no chairs or tables, standing on their feet, jammed together, energizing each other."[9]

During the late nineties, he performed on the same bill as up-and-coming country and folk acts like Jewel and Wilco, as well as performers like Shawn Colvin and Patty Griffin. Having all those young acts paired with Cash allowed a whole new generation of fans—fans who called the music they listened to "alt-country"—to discover not only Johnny Cash, but June Carter Cash, as well, boosting their future album sales—and their place in the history of American music.

including "Rowboat" by Beck and "Rusty Cage," first recorded by Soundgarden, mixed with three new Cash compositions and some songs from the fifties and sixties.

The Struggle Continues

Recording was a slow process. Cash's broken jaw required numerous operations. Worse, he had begun stumbling and shaking to the point where he was sometimes unable to sing.

But when *Unchained* came out in November 1996, it placed fifth on *Rolling Stone*'s list of the Ten Best Albums of 1996. In December, Cash received a Kennedy Center Lifetime Achievement Award. In February 1998, *Unchained* won the Grammy for Best Country Album. The following year, Cash received a Lifetime Achievement Award at

Cash (second from right) and wife June Carter (fifth from left) perform onstage with their band in 1994. Cash and Carter performed together hundreds of times during their marriage.

the Grammy ceremony. Cash's second autobiography, co-written with Patrick Carr, came out in 1997.

His personal struggles only intensified. His daughter Rosanne remembers having lunch in New York with Cash, June, Rosanne's husband, John, and her two daughters after *Unchained* came out. Cash started hallucinating, imagining black puppies in the room. He spilled orange juice in his lap. Rosanne thinks he was once again abusing pain medication. "It was kind of like that until his death," she said. "He would be lucid, and then he would kind of drift off."[10]

In October 1997, Cash wrote in the paperback version of his autobiography, he suddenly found himself walking backward on a street in New York. A doctor told Cash he needed to go home and into the hospital right away.[11]

On October 25, in Flint, Michigan, Cash almost collapsed as he bent over to pick up a guitar pick. He announced to the audience that he had Parkinson's Disease, a slow-progressing disease of the nervous system that impairs movement and over time can make it difficult to walk, talk, or perform other simple tasks. Some laughed, thinking he was joking. He wasn't.

That was the last full-length concert Johnny Cash ever gave.[12]

Cash entered Nashville's Baptist Hospital on October 29. He was diagnosed with a combination of pneumonia, diabetes, and nerve damage. He lapsed into a coma for twelve days. June arranged for a special prayer request to be posted to the Johnny Cash website.[13]

The next morning, Cash woke up and asked for coffee.

Now doctors told him he had something worse than Parkinson's: Shy-Drager syndrome, which affects the brain and nervous system and usually ends in death a few years after symptoms develop. They put his life expectancy at no more than eighteen months.[14]

The paperback version of his autobiography included his thoughts on the diagnosis: "I don't have any fear of death," he wrote. "I'm very much at peace with myself and my God. . .I have no regrets, I carry no guilt, and I bear no ill will toward anybody."[15]

The Final Years

Despite what seemed like a death sentence, Cash and June headed off to Jamaica in early December. Six months later, in June 1998, Cash made a surprise appearance at a Kris Kristofferson tribute in Nashville, singing "Sunday Morning Coming Down" with Kristofferson. But mostly he stayed out of public view. That fall he ended up in the hospital with pneumonia again. Released after ten days, he suffered a relapse and returned to the hospital for most of October.

During that difficult year, Cash began talking to producer James Keach about a movie version of his life, to be called *Walk the Line*. Cash and June had become friends with Keach, the husband of actress Jane Seymour, when they had guest-starred in several episodes Seymour's show, *Doctor Quinn, Medicine Woman*. Keach said Cash thought he would make the movie about more than just "sex and drugs and rock-'n'-roll," and would recognize "his journey as a man and his love with June and the fact that God was at the core of his story."[1]

Cash worked closely with scriptwriter Gil Denis on a script, which originally sold to Sony and eventually ended up with Fox 2000, but Cash didn't live to see the film made.

The Beginning of the End

In April 1999, Cash took part in a television tribute to his music that included performances by Bruce Springsteen, U2, Emmylou Harris, and Wyclef Jean, with Jean's hip-hop performance emphasizing the link young listeners had found between Cash's image as a rebel and the spirit of rebelliousness inherent in hip-hop.

Cash sang "Folsom Prison Blues" and "I Walk the Line." For the first time in nineteen years, Marshall Grant played bass. "He looked road-ready," said biographer Michael Streissguth, but that was the last performance Cash gave to any audience of a significant size.[2]

Johnny Cash is surrounded by friends and fellow musicians during a special tribute concert in his honor in 1999 at New York City's Hammerstein Ballroom.

He didn't stop working, though. He provided songs for the soundtracks of the movies *We Were Soldiers* and *Dead Men Walking*, and more songs to tribute albums for the Louvin Brothers and Hank Williams. He completed a third album for American Records, *Solitary Man*, released in 2000. Cash wrote three of the songs, co-wrote another, and co-adapted a fourth. Other songs included Neil Diamond's "Solitary Man" and Tom Petty's "I Won't Back Down." Critical response was positive, but Cash's voice was noticeably weaker.

JUNE GOES SOLO

In 1999, June released only the second solo album of her career, *Press On*. (The first, *Appalachian Pride*, came out in the 1970s.) *Press On* mixed Carter Family songs with some that June co-wrote, and it won the Grammy for Best Traditional Folk Album in 2000. Cash sang on some numbers.

Asked by a reporter if she'd be touring, June said, "If we go back on the road, we'll go together. I'll go where he goes, and he'll go where I go."[6]

They never toured again, but June did record a third solo album, *Wildwood Flower*, another mix of Carter Family songs and June's originals, with June and Cash singing together on two songs. Released posthumously in 2003, it won Grammys for Best Female Country Vocal Performance and Best Traditional Folk Album in 2004.

Rubin reassured the frustrated Cash that it "didn't sound as though he were tired, it sounded like he was emoting."[3] He said, "If there was a bad day, we would circle back to the material a couple of days later and get a great take."[4] Rosanne Cash later said her father's health "would have gone down like a forty-five-degree angle" if he hadn't been recording with Rubin.[5]

Recording was interrupted twice in October 1999 by two trips to the hospital, first for a gash in his leg, and then for pneumonia. During the second stay, doctors had good news: Cash didn't have the fatal Shy-Drager syndrome, but a non-fatal autonomic neuropathy. His symptoms were caused by damage to the part of the nervous system that controls the bodily functions we don't have to think about: breathing, sweating, balance, etc.

Cash continued collecting and writing songs for yet another album. He said he spent more time on what became the title song, "The Man Comes Around," than any other song he ever wrote. Focused on the prophesied second coming of Jesus Christ, it was full of apocalyptic images from the Bible.

Recording was more challenging than ever. Cash's eyesight had begun to fail, so the lyrics had to be printed in large boldface type.

Cash Gets "Hurt"

One of the best songs on the new album was "Hurt." Written by Trent Reznor for Nine Inch Nails, it's about a heroin addict who hurts himself and everyone around him. Its somber lyrics, Rick Rubin said, resonated with Cash. "I imagined him singing it and knew how powerful it could be."[7]

Once again Cash mixed new material (like "Hurt") with his own songs (like "The Man Comes Around"), traditional songs (such as "Danny Boy"), and old standards (including "We'll Meet Again," a World War II classic by British singer Vera Lynn). He even included a Beatles song, "In My Life."

The cover photos emphasized Cash's frailty. And then there was the poignant video for "Hurt," in which images of Cash performing the song with June Carter standing nearby were intercut with film of when he was younger. Images of the closed Cash Museum, recently damaged by a flood, emphasized the idea of decay and loss.

When Rosanne Cash saw "Hurt" in Cash's office, she said, "I was devastated. I was crying like a baby." She told her father it was "the most powerful video I had ever seen."[8] But she noted Cash and June viewed it dispassionately. During filming, Cash reportedly joked with the crew between takes.

On October 17, 2002, the day before the filming, June was diagnosed with a leaking heart valve.[9]

The Man Comes Around came out on November 4, 2002. By then, Cash and June were in Jamaica, their custom every winter.

The video for "Hurt" was released in early 2003. *Rolling Stone* called it "one of the most intense and affecting videos in the history of MTV."[10] The album sold more than a million copies, Cash's first studio-recorded album to go platinum.

In January, Cash was back in the hospital in Nashville, once again with pneumonia. In February, he was back again, after cutting his knee. In March, he was admitted after he fell out of bed and passed out. This time, when he was released, for the first time ever, he had to ride out in a wheelchair, and use a walker thereafter.

When Cash's sister Louise died two days later, Cash was too ill to attend her funeral.

Farewell to June

With Cash too unwell to attend, June Carter Cash accepted an award for "Hurt" on behalf of her husband

Country singer Vince Gill presents June Carter with her husband's lifetime achievement award at the 2003 CMT Flameworthy Awards. Cash was too ill to accept the award himself.

at the 2003 CMT Flameworthy Video Music Awards. But she wasn't doing well, either; she looked unwell and had trouble delivering her lines.[11]

On April 11, she was rushed to hospital and diagnosed with congestive heart failure. After a few days, doctors sent her home, but twelve days later, she was back.

Doctors decided her only hope was to replace her defective heart valve. They operated on May 7. By the next day, June was breathing on her own. Cash spent several hours with her, talking about what they would do when she was out of the hospital, and how he planned to work hard so he could walk unassisted again.

But after Cash left, June called Kathy, Cash's second-oldest daughter. She told her she didn't feel she was going to make it and to "please take care of Daddy."[12] Kathy didn't tell her father what June had said, not wanting to worry him.

Early the next morning, June suffered cardiac arrest. Doctors resuscitated her, but it took twenty minutes, and she remained in a coma. The family gathered. Tests showed no brain activity, due to lack of oxygen during the resuscitation attempt. Cash gathered the family in a circle. They prayed. Then Cash gave his permission for the life support system to be switched off.

June Carter Cash died three days later.[13]

Working Through the Grief

Cash turned to work for solace. He recorded more songs and experimented with new sounds. But he found life without June very difficult. He had her photos and letters enlarged so he could see them, and the cover of her *Wildwood Flower* album painted on the elevator in the

A FINAL FAREWELL

Around 1,800 people attended June's public funeral at First Baptist Church in Hendersonville, broadcast live on local television. Larry Gatlin, Emmylou Harris, Sheryl Crow, the Oak Ridge Boys, and others performed gospel songs.

Rosanne Cash, the only member of the family to speak, said, "My daddy has lost his dearest companion, his musical counterpart, his soul mate and best friend."[14]

June would be followed in death not only by her beloved husband of thirty-five years, but by her forty-five-year-old daughter Rosie, who passed away in October that year from accidental carbon monoxide poisoning.

house. He would pick up the telephone and pretend to talk to her.

Cindy Cash came for what she thought would be a short visit in June, and ended up staying with her father until his death. All his daughters stayed close to him those final weeks. "We had some beautiful conversations," Rosanne remembered. "Some of the best conversations of my life."[15]

On June 22, the day before June's birthday, Cash travelled to Hiltons, Virginia, the hometown of the Carter Family, and performed for a thousand people at the

Carter Fold. Two weeks later, he returned and performed another seven songs, interrupting a local bluegrass band.

"Despite being crippled, hoarse, short of breath mid-song and profoundly depressed, Cash knew he could still thrill an audience," wrote Randy Noles, consulting publisher for *Sarasota Magazine*, who was in the audience that day.[16]

A week later, Vivian Cash paid him a visit, seeking permission to write a book based on the letters they'd exchanged while he was in the Air Force. Cash agreed. "It's time," he told her. He said he hoped they would be healing for her, and even promised to write the foreword. They hugged. "I never stopped loving him," she wrote later. "Through all of it, despite everything, I never stopped loving him for one second."[17]

By August, Cash was nearly blind. But when Cindy Cash and Cash's sister Reba took him to see June's grave one day, he managed to read the stone and told her, "I'm coming, baby."[18]

After another stay in hospital that month, Cash started working with a sports physician, Phil Maffetone. With a change of diet and a new physical therapy program, Cash was soon walking better than he had in months. He hoped to attend the MTV Music Awards in New York on August 28 ("Hurt" was nominated for Video of the Year), and booked a flight to Los Angeles for afterward, planning to resume recording with Rubin.

But MTV told Lou Robin ahead of time that "Hurt" was not going to win video of the year. Cash wouldn't have made the event anyway. He returned to the hospital on Monday, August 24, suffering from peritonitis, and stayed there until September 9.

Johnny Cash's casket is carried by family members and friends following his funeral on September 15, 2003. Cash died of respiratory failure on September 12, at age 71.

Fade to Black

Two days later, at home, Cash was working with Maffetone when he suddenly said, "It's time." Maffetone, thinking Cash was just tired, went back to his hotel.[19]

But in fact, Cash's damaged lungs were failing. By afternoon, he was delirious and coughing blood. Although he was conscious after arriving at the hospital, he couldn't talk. He squeezed the hands of his children John Carter,

99

Kathy, and Rosanne. In the middle of the night they were wakened to return to their father's room. The three of them comforted him as best they could; and then, at 2 a.m., on September 12, 2003, Johnny Cash died.

The private funeral at First Baptist Church featured some of the same musicians who had performed at June's funeral. Emmylou Harris and Sheryl Crow were there. Franklin Graham represented his father, Billy Graham. Kris Kristofferson called Cash "Abraham Lincoln with a wild side."[20]

Cash was buried next to June. Engraved on his grave marker is his name, the dates of his birth and death, and Psalm 19:14: "Let the words of my mouth and the meditation of my heart be acceptable in thy sight, O Lord, my strength, and my redeemer."

Beneath that is Cash's signature.

CONCLUSION

November 2003 saw the release of *Unearthed*, a boxed set of five CDs with an accompanying, lavishly illustrated book that included notes on the songs. It seemed the perfect capstone to Cash's career, featuring seventy-seven songs Cash had recorded with Rick Rubin over the previous decade, most never before released. The tracks ran the gamut from hymns Cash had learned from his mother as a child to songs by Bob Marley, Neil Young, and Steve Earle. For the most part, critics welcomed the set, although some accused Rubin of milking Cash's final years.[1]

That same month, a televised tribute aired, hosted by Tim Robbins and featuring taped appearances by people as diverse as Whoopi Goldberg, Billy Graham, and Dan Rather.

Tributes poured in. New York's *Village Voice* called Cash "the most important country artist of the modern era."[2] England's *Guardian* newspaper called him a singer whose work would endure indefinitely.[3] Britain's *Time Out* said, "If America as a nation could speak. . .it would sound something like Johnny Cash."[4]

In a special commemorative issue of *Rolling Stone*, Bob Dylan called Cash "the greatest of the great then and now," adding, "Blessed with a profound imagination, he used the gift to express all the various lost causes of the human soul. Listen to him, and he always brings you to your senses."[5]

Jerry Lee Lewis remembered touring with Carl Perkins and Johnny Cash in 1956. "Elvis and them were rockabilly; I was rock & roll," Lewis said. "But. . .if you break it down to the nitty-gritty, we're all country people. We were called rebels—I guess because we were."[6]

The Legacy of Johnny Cash

In 2005, the movie version of Cash's early life, *Walk the Line*, starring Joaquin Phoenix as Cash and Reese Witherspoon as June Carter, was successful both critically and financially. Nominated for five Academy Awards, it won one: Witherspoon took home the Oscar for Best Performance by an Actress in a Leading Role.

In the movie, Ginnifer Goodwin played Cash's first wife, Vivian. The real-life Vivian died just a few months before the movie came out, on May 24, 2005. Two months before, on March 12, *Ring of Fire*, created by Richard Maltby, Jr., and featuring the music of Johnny Cash, opened at the Ethel Barrymore Theatre on Broadway. Cash had given the stage rights to his life story and music to producer Bill Meade just before he died. Although it only ran for thirty-eight performances on Broadway, *Ring of Fire* continues to be performed all over the country.

In 2006, Barry Gibb of the Bee Gees bought Cash's former house and property in Hendersonville for $2.3 million, but the house burned to the ground in April 2007.[7] Texas businessman James Gresham bought the estate in 2014 and put it up for sale in November, 2016[8]; as of March 2017, it was still on the market.

That same year, *American V: A Hundred Highways*, the first posthumous album produced by Rick Rubin, was released. It included Cash's final composition, a "train-song-as-meditation-on-mortality" called "Like the 309." *American VI: Ain't No Grave* came out in February 2010. Debuting at number three on the US Billboard 200 chart, it became Cash's third posthumous top-ten album in the US.

The other Cash albums released since his death have been compilations—except for two drawn from hundreds of hours of tapes found in the Hendersonville archives and catalogued by producer Gregg Geller and Cash's son, John Carter Cash. The 2006 two-CD set, *Personal*

Reese Witherspoon and Joaquin Phoenix portray June Carter and Johnny Cash, respectively, in the 2005 biopic, *Walk the Line*. Witherspoon won an Oscar for her potrayal of June.

File, featured forty-nine previously unissued solo Cash tracks, half of them from a July 1973 recording session. A second album, *More Songs from Johnny's Personal File,* was released in 2007.

Every year sees more tributes to Cash. In October 2016, the Rock & Roll Hall of Fame (into which Cash was inducted in 1992) honored him as its Annual Music Master. A week of events included a tribute concert that featured performers who ran the gamut from punk rockers to the Oak Ridge Boys. John Carter Cash served as the executive bandleader.

Another place where Cash's legacy is being cemented is in the very place his story began: Dyess, Arkansas. The

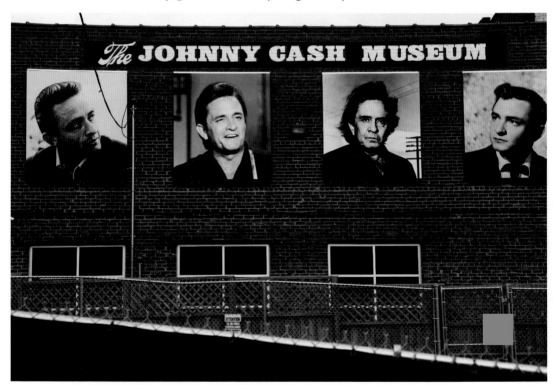

The Johnny Cash Museum, dedicated to the life and recordings of country music's most famous outlaw, opened in 2013 in downtown Nashville, Tennessee.

first Johnny Cash Heritage Festival was set for Dyess in October 2017. Rosanne Cash worked with Arkansas State University to arrange festival. "We foresee an annual festival that will include both world-renowned artists on the main stage and local musicians on smaller stages, as well as educational panels, exhibits and local crafts," she said when the festival was announced.[9]

The festival grew out of a four-year series of concerts in Jonesboro, Arkansas, to raise funds for the restoration of Cash's boyhood home in Dyess, which opened to the public in August 2014, along with exhibits about the New Deal colony, and its impact on Cash, in the historic Dyess Colony Administration Building.

November 2016 saw the publication of a collection of Cash's poetry, *Forever Words: The Unknown Poems*, selected by John Carter Cash with the help of author Paul Muldoon. An associated album was in the works, with artists like Brad Paisley, T Bone Burnett and Jewel taking the poems and setting them to music.

John Carter Cash told *Rolling Stone* his father's true legacy is the message he sought to convey, "what he believed in, what he stood for, the understanding of his own darkness, the faith that he had that drove him, and the great love that he had for people."[10]

As Kris Kristofferson put it after Cash's death, "He was willing and able to be the champion of people who didn't have one."[11]

The legacy of this rebel with a cause will live on forever.

CHRONOLOGY

1932 J.R. Cash is born in Kingsland, Arkansas, on February 26.

1935 Cash and family move to Dyess, Arkansas.

1950 Cash graduates from Dyess High School and enlists in the United States Air Force.

1954 Receives an honorable discharge at Camp Kilmer, New Jersey; in July, he moves to Memphis, Tennessee; on August 7, he marries Vivian Liberto in San Antonio, Texas.

1955 Cash's first child, Rosanne Cash, is born in Memphis; on June 21, his first single is released.

1956 On April 2, Cash records "I Walk the Line"; on April 16, second child, Kathy Cash, is born in Memphis; on July 7, Cash debuts on Grand Ole Opry, where he meets June Carter.

1958 July 29, third child, Cindy Cash, is born in Memphis; on August 1, he starts a new contract with Columbia Records.

1959 On January 1, Cash plays San Quentin Prison in California for the first time; on February 23, he's featured in Time magazine.

1960 In June, Cash has his first movie appearance in *Five Minutes to Live*; on August 5, drummer W. S. "Fluke" Holland joins the band, turning the Tennessee Two into the Tennessee Three.

1961 In July, Saul Holiff takes over from Stew Carnall as manager; on August 24, fourth child, Tara Cash, is born in Encino, California.

1962 On February 11, June Carter joins *The Johnny Cash Show*.

1964 On July 26, he plays the Newport Folk Festival.

1966 On June 30, Vivian Liberto Cash begins divorce proceedings.

1968 On January 3, Cash and Vivian's divorce is finalized; on January 13, he records the concert at Folsom Prison, California; on March 1, he marries June in Franklin, Kentucky.

1970 On March 3, Cash's fifth child, John Carter Cash, is born; on April 17, he plays the White House as a guest of President Richard Nixon.

1975 In August, Cash publishes his first autobiography, *Man in Black*.

1977 In May, Cash is awarded an associate degree of theology by Christian International School of Theology; on August 16, he is ordained as a Christian minister.

1980 On October 13, Cash is inducted into the Country Music Hall of Fame.

1985 On December 23, his father, Ray Cash, dies at age eighty-eight.

1988 On December 12, a routine checkup detects that Cash has blocked arteries; on December 19, he is hospitalized for bypass surgery.

1991 On February 20, Cash wins the Living Legend Award at the Grammys; on March 11, his mother, Carrie Cash, dies at age eighty-six; on May 1, the creation of Cash Country in Branson, Missouri, is announced.

1992 On January 15, Cash is inducted into the Rock and Roll Hall of Fame; in May, the failure of Cash Country is announced.

1995 In February, *American Recordings* wins the Grammy for Best Contemporary Folk Album; on May 4, Cash cancels his European tour due to complications from jaw surgery.

1996 In November, *Unchained*, Cash's second album with Rick Rubin, is released.

1997 On September 16, Cash tells his band he plans to retire; on October 15, *Cash: The Autobiography* is published; on October 25, Cash performs his final concert in Flint, Michigan.

1998 In February, *Unchained* wins the Grammy for Best Country Album; on August 6, Cash is hospitalized for four days.

1999 In January, Cash receives the Lifetime Achievement Award at the Grammys; on April 6, the All-Star Tribute to Johnny Cash takes place in New York; on October 20, Cash is hospitalized with pneumonia.

2000 In January, Cash starts recording his third album with Rick Rubin; on April 23, Cash receives a Living Legend Medal from the Library of Congress; on May 23, the triple CD compilation *Love, God, Murder* is released by Legacy; on October 17, *Solitary Man* is released.

2001 In February, Cash is hospitalized with pneumonia; on February 21, Cash wins his

tenth Grammy, for Best Male Country Vocal
Performance.

On October 11, Cash films *Larry King Live*;
on October 17, June's leaking heart valve is
detected; October 18–19, the video for "Hurt"
is shot in Hendersonville; on November 4, *The
Man Comes Around* is released.

On May 15, June Carter Cash dies of surgical
complications; on September 12, Johnny Cash
dies of respiratory problems.

The movie *Walk the Line*, about Cash's life,
opens.

The Johnny Cash Museum opens in Nashville.

The Storytellers Museum opens in Johnny
Cash's old ranch in Bon Aqua, Tennessee.

CHAPTER NOTES

Introduction

1. Kot, Greg. "A Critical Discography." Cash: by the Editors of Rolling Stone. New York: Crown Publishers, 2004, p. 188.

Chapter 1: Born into Hard Times

1. PBS.org. "The American Experience: Surviving the Dust Bowl: The Great Depression." < http://www.pbs.org/wgbh/amex/dustbowl/peopleevents/pandeAMEX05.html>, (May 16, 2008).

2. Turner, Steve. The Man Called Cash. Nashville, TN: W Publishing Group, 2004, p. 17.

3. Gross, Terry. "Interview with Johnny Cash." Fresh Air (National Public Radio), August 21, 1998.

4. Cash, Johnny, with Carr, Patrick. Johnny Cash: The Autobiography. New York: HarperCollins, 1997, p. 5.

5. Turner, p. 17.

6. Cash and Carr, p. 13.

7. Harrington, Richard. "Walking the Line; Johnny Cash's Craggy Legend," The Washington Post, December 8, 1996.

8. Cash, Johnny. Man in Black. Grand Rapids, MI: Zondervan, 1975, p.24.

9. Streissguth, Michael. Johnny Cash: the biography. Cambridge: Da Capo Press, 2006, p. 13.

10. Ibid, p. 16.

11. Cash and Carr, pp. 237-238.

12. Turner, p. 20.

13. Cash and Carr, p. 71.

14. Cash, p. 34.

15. Ibid, p. 38.

16. Cash and Carr, p. 37.

17. Ibid, p. 23.

Chapter 2: Birth of the Music

1. Turner, Steve. The Man Called Cash. Nashville, TN: W
   Publishing Group, 2004, p. 25.

2. Cash, Johnny, with Carr, Patrick. Johnny Cash: The
   Autobiography. New York: HarperCollins, 1997, p. 50.

3. Gross, Terry. "Interview with Johnny Cash." Fresh Air
   (National Public Radio), August 21, 1998.

4. Cash and Carr, p. 53.

5. Gross.

6. Gilmore, Mikal. "Man in Black." Cash: by the Editors of
   Rolling Stone. New York: Crown Publishers, 2004, p 27.

7. Turner, p. 27.

8. Ibid.

9. Ibid, p. 28.

10. Ibid, p. 26.

11. Streissguth, Michael. Johnny Cash: the biography.
    Cambridge: Da Capo Press, 2006, p. 27.

12. Wren, Christopher S. Winners Got Scars Too: The Life
    of Johnny Cash. New York: Dial Press, 1971.

13. Gilmore.

14. Salamon, Ed. "Johnny Cash Tells the Stories Behind His
    Greatest Hits." Country Music, July/August 1980.

15. Cash, Johnny. Man in Black. Grand Rapids, MI:
    Zondervan, 1975, pp.67-68.

16. Turner, p. 38.

17. Turner, p. 47.

18. Cash, p. 70.

19. Ibid, p. 72.

20. "The Sun Story." Sun Records. < http://www. sunrecords.com/content/view/61/75/1/0/>, (May 17, 2008).

21. Gross.

22. Ibid.

23. Turner, p. 53.

24. Ibid, pp. 52-54.

Chapter 3: Here Come the Hits

1. Cash, Johnny. Man in Black. Grand Rapids, MI: Zondervan, 1975, p. 79.

2. Cash, p. 80.

3. Gross, Terry. "Interview with Johnny Cash." Fresh Air (National Public Radio), August 21, 1998.

4. Gilmore, Mikal. "Man in Black." Cash: by the Editors of Rolling Stone. New York: Crown Publishers, 2004, p 32.

5. Cash, p. 88.

6. Streissguth, Michael. Johnny Cash: the biography. Cambridge: Da Capo Press, 2006, p. 71.

7. Cash, p. 85.

8. Ibid., p. 87.

9. Streissguth, p. 71.

10. Turner, p. 61.

11. Perlich, Tim. "Johnny Cash: Hard-living Legend Finds Youthful Alternative to Nashville Grind." New Magazine, November 21-27, 1996.

12. Harrington, Richard. "Walking the Line: Johnny Cash's Craggy Legend." The Washington Post, December 8, 1996.

13. Turner, p. 67.

14. Green, Ben A. "Johnny Cash Achieves 'Life's Ambition,' Wins Opry Heart." Nashville Banner, July 16, 1956.

15. Ibid.

16. Pond, Steve. "Johnny Cash: The Rolling Stone Interview." Rolling Stone, December 10-24, 1992.

17. Cash, John Carter. Anchored in Love: An Intimate Portrait of June Carter Cash. Nashville: Thomas Nelson, 2007, p. 45.

18. Cash, June Carter. Liner notes, Johnny Cash: Love God Murder, Sony Music, 2000.

19. Gleason, Ralph J. "It Looks As Though Elvis Has A Rival--From Arkansas," San Francisco Chronicle, December 16, 1956.

20. Johnson, Robert. "Gleason Signs Cash for 10 Guest Spots." Memphis Press-Scimitar, January 7, 1957.

21. Turner, pp. 71-72.

22. Ibid, p. 73

23. Cash, p. 91.

Chapter 4: Sliding Downhill

1. Cash, Johnny. Man in Black. Grand Rapids, MI: Zondervan, 1975, p. 75.

2. Streissguth, Michael. Johnny Cash: the biography. Cambridge: Da Capo Press, 2006, p. 90.

3. Cash, Johnny, with Carr, Patrick. Johnny Cash: The Autobiography. New York: HarperCollins, 1997, p. 84.

4. Escott, Colin and Hawkins, Martin. Good Rockin' Tonight: Sun Records and the Birth of Rock 'n' Roll. (New York: St. Martin's Press, 1991). p. 26.

5. Ibid.

6. "Write is Wrong." Time Magazine, February 23, 1959.

7. Streissguth, pp. 95-97.

8. Dylan, Bob. "Remembering Johnny Cash." Cash: by the Editors of Rolling Stone. New York: Crown Publishers, 2004, p 205.

9. Turner, p. 82.

10. Cash, Johnny. Man in Black. Grand Rapids, MI: Zondervan, 1975, p. 93.

11. Cash and Carr, p. 145.

12. Ibid.

13. Streissguth, p. 98.

14. Turner, pp. 87-89.

Chapter 5: Down and Out and Up Again

1. Cash, Johnny. Man in Black. Grand Rapids, MI: Zondervan, 1975, p. 138.

2. Ibid, p. 130.

3. Ibid, p. 116.

4. Ibid, pp. 116-117.

5. Ibid, p. 118

6. Streissguth, p. 133.

7. Turner, p. 119.

8. Turner, p. 120.

9. Cash, p. 140.

10. Cash, Johnny, with Carr, Patrick. Johnny Cash: The Autobiography. New York: HarperCollins, 1997, p. 174.

11. Cash and Carr, p. 235.

12. Kot, Greg. "A Critical Discography." Cash: by the Editors of Rolling Stone. New York: Crown Publishers, 2004. p. 188.

13. Cash and Carr, p. 173.

14. Morris, W.R. "Legend Credits Guitarist Established Sound." Music City News, May, 1979.

15. Streissguth, p. 158.

16. Turner, p. 135.

17. Gleason, Ralph J. "Johnny Cash at San Quentin." Rolling Stone, May 31, 1969.

18. Streissguth, p. 160.

19. Turner, p. 135.

20. Simon, Marion. "Smart Money says Johnny Cash Is the One to Watch This Year." National Observer, June 2, 1969.

21. Turner, p. 136.

22. Dearmore, Tom. "First Angry Man of Country Singers." New York Times Magazine, September 21, 1969.

23. Turner, pp. 138-139.

24. Ibid, p. 142.

25. Cash and Carr, p. 206

26. Streissguth, pp. 170-172.

27. Turner, p. 141.

28. Cash and Carr, p. 207.

Chapter 6: Rock Bottom

1. Turner, Steve. The Man Called Cash. Nashville, TN: W Publishing Group, 2004, p. 145.

2. Ibid, p. 146.

3. Cash, Johnny, with Carr, Patrick. Johnny Cash: The Autobiography. New York: HarperCollins, 1997, p. 228.

4. Streissguth, p. 184.

5. Hillburn, Robert. "Nothing Can Take the Place of the Human Heart: A Conversation with Johnny Cash." Rolling Stone, March 1, 1975.

6. Turner, p. 150.

7. Turner, p. 161.

8. Ibid, p. 158.

9. Streissguth, p. 204.

10. Streissguth, p. 204.

11. Turner, p. 167.

12. Ibid, p. 168.

13. Cash and Carr, p. 250.

14. Ibid, p. 251.

15. Turner, p. 172.

16. Ibid, p. 175.

17. Cash and Carr, p. 183.

18. Ibid, p. 239.

19. Ibid, p. 237.

20. Turner, p. 179.

21. Oermann, Robert K. "Reporter's Aim Was in Wrong Direction." The Tennessean, July 21, 1986.

22. Cash and Carr, p. 251.

23. Flanagan, Bill. "Johnny Cash. American." Musician, May 1988.

Chapter 7: A New Audience

1. Turner, Steve. The Man Called Cash. Nashville, TN: W Publishing Group, 2004, p. 187.

2. Streissguth, Michael. Johnny Cash: the biography. Cambridge: Da Capo Press, 2006, p. 236.

3. Bono. "Remembering Johnny Cash." Cash: by the Editors of Rolling Stone. New York: Crown Publishers, 2004. p. 208.

4. Turner, p. 190.

5. Cash and Carr, p. 253.

6. Ibid, p. 254.

7. Fricke, David. "Rick Rubin: The Rolling Stone Interview." Cash: by the Editors of Rolling Stone. New York: Crown Publishers, 2004, p. 146.

8. Cash and Carr, p. 255.

9. Ibid, p. 256.

10. Striessguth, p. 265.

11. Cash and Carr, revised paperback edition, p. 400.

12. Turner, p. 204.

13. Ibid.

14. Ibid, p. 205.

15. Cash and Carr, paperback, p. 402.

Chapter 8: The Final Years

1. Turner, p. 208.

2. Streissguth, p. 271.

3. Turner, p. 211.

4. Fricke.

5. Streissguth, p. 272

6. Arnold, Gina. "She Walked the Line for You Johnny." The Scotsman, May 20, 1999,

7. Fricke.

8. Turner, p. 216.

9. Ibid, p. 3.

10. Binellli, Mark. "Screen Life: Cash's Greatest Film & TV Moment." Cash: by the Editors of Rolling Stone. New York: Crown Publishers, 2004. p. 203.

11. Turner, p. 4.

12. Ibid, pp. 5-6.

13. Ibid, p. 7.

14. Ibid, p. 11.

15. Streissguth, p. 285.

16. Noles, Randy. "Unbroken circle: a frail and grieving Johnny Cash inspired consulting publisher Randy Noles and other spellbound fans at his final concert in Appalachia." Sarasota Magazine. October 1, 2003.

17. Cash, Vivian, with Sharpsteen, Ann. I Walked the Line. New York: Scribner. 2007. p. 8.

18. Streissguth, pp. 283-284.

19. Streissguth, p. 289.

20. Turner, p. 222.

Conclusion

1. Ibid, p. 224.

2. Smucker, Tom. "Johnny Cash, 1932—2003: Cowboy and Indian, Sinner and Believer, Patriot and Protester, the Man in Black Walks his Final Line." The Village Voice. September 16, 2003

3. Simmons, Sylvie. "Hello. I'm Johnny Cash." Guardian. September 19, 2003.

4. Fortune, Ross. Obituary. Time Out. September 17-24, 2003.

5. "Remembering Johnny." Rolling Stone. < http://www.rollingstone.com/artists/johnnycash/articles/story/5940093/remembering_johnny>. (May 15, 2008.)

6. Ibid.

7. Usborne, David. "Johnny's House, Destroyed by a Ring of Fire." The Independent. April 12, 2007. < http://www.highbeam.com/doc/1P2-5856041.html>, (May 15, 2008.)

8. Ward, Getahn. "Johnny Cash's former lakefront Hendersonville estate up for sale." The Tennessean, November 17, 2016. http://www.tennessean.com/story/money/real-estate/2016/11/17/johnny-cashs-former-lakefront-hendersonville-estate-up-sale/94022938/, (March 29, 2017).

9. "Johnny Cash Heritage Festival to Begin in 2017." News article, Arkansas State University, May 21, 2016. < http://www.astate.edu/news/johnny-cash-heritage-festival-to-begin-in-2017>, (March 29, 2017).

10. Hodge, Will. "Johnny Cash: Inside the Country Legend's Forgotten Poetry." Rolling Stone, November 21, 2016. http://www.rollingstone.com/country/news/johnny-cash-inside-the-country-legends-forgotten-poetry-w451635, (March 29, 2017).

11. Ibid.

GLOSSARY

acoustic guitar   A guitar whose sound is amplified only by its own body, not by any electronic means.

album   A collection of recorded songs.

amphetamine   A type of drug that stimulates the nervous system.

concept album   An album whose songs are all built around a particular musical or lyrical theme.

cotton gin   Machinery for removing the seeds from the fibrous balls of cotton plucked from the the plant.

country chart   A list, compiled weekly, of the top-selling recordings of country songs.

electric guitar   A guitar whose sound is amplified electronically.

folk music   Music either directly drawn from or based on music that has been passed down generation to generation by memorization rather than by writing.

gig   Show business slang for a performance.

Gospel music   Music with an explicitly Christiann theme, often based on traditional folk music.

Grand Ole Opry   A weekly country music radio program and concert broadcast live from Nashville that is the oldest continuous radio program in the United States, having begun in 1925.

live album   An album recorded at a live concert, as opposed to being recorded in a studio.

manager   The person who oversees a musician's career, booking concerts, arranging tours, and negotiating contracts.

painkillers   Drugs designed to ease pain.

pop chart   A list, compiled weekly, of the top-selling recordings of pop songs.

riding the rails   Jumping aboard a boxcar to get a free train ride to another city where work might be found.

riff   A repeated chord progression, pattern, refrain, or melody.

rockabilly   One of the earliest forms of rock and roll. The name is a mixture of rock and hillbilly, or country, music.

royalty   The percentage of the money earned from the sale of each record that is paid to the artist.

single   A song released to radio on its own, not necessarily as part of an album, although often used to promote an album.

studio   A special room fitted with microphones, recording equipment, and everything else needed to make a record.

FURTHER READING

Books

Cash, John Carter. *House of Cash: The Legacies of My Father, Johnny Cash*. New York, NY: Insight Editions, 2015.

Cash, Johnny. *Forever Words: The Unknown Poems*. New York, NY: Blue Rider Press, 2016.

Hillburn, Robert. *Johnny Cash: The Life*. New York, NY: Little, Brown and Company, 2013.

Websites

Johnny Cash Museum

www.johnnycashmuseum.com
A Nashville-based museum that honors Johnny Cash, the website contains information on the museum as well as on Cash's life and music.

Johnny Cash Online

www.johnnycashonline.com
The official website for Johnny Cash, it features a biography and discography, up-to-date news on Cash's estate, as well as videos and audio clips.

Rolling Stone: Johnny Cash

www.rollingstone.com/artists/johnnycash
Music news magazine Rolling Stone's archive of articles about Johnny Cash.

Film

Borofsky, Michael B. *The Johnny Cash Show: The Best of Johnny Cash 1969–1971*. Sony Columbia Legacy, 2007.

Mangold, James. *Walk the Line*. 20th Century Fox, 2005.

Tappis, Jordan and Derik Murray. *Johnny Cash: American Rebel*. CMT, 2015.

INDEX